# Fart Waves

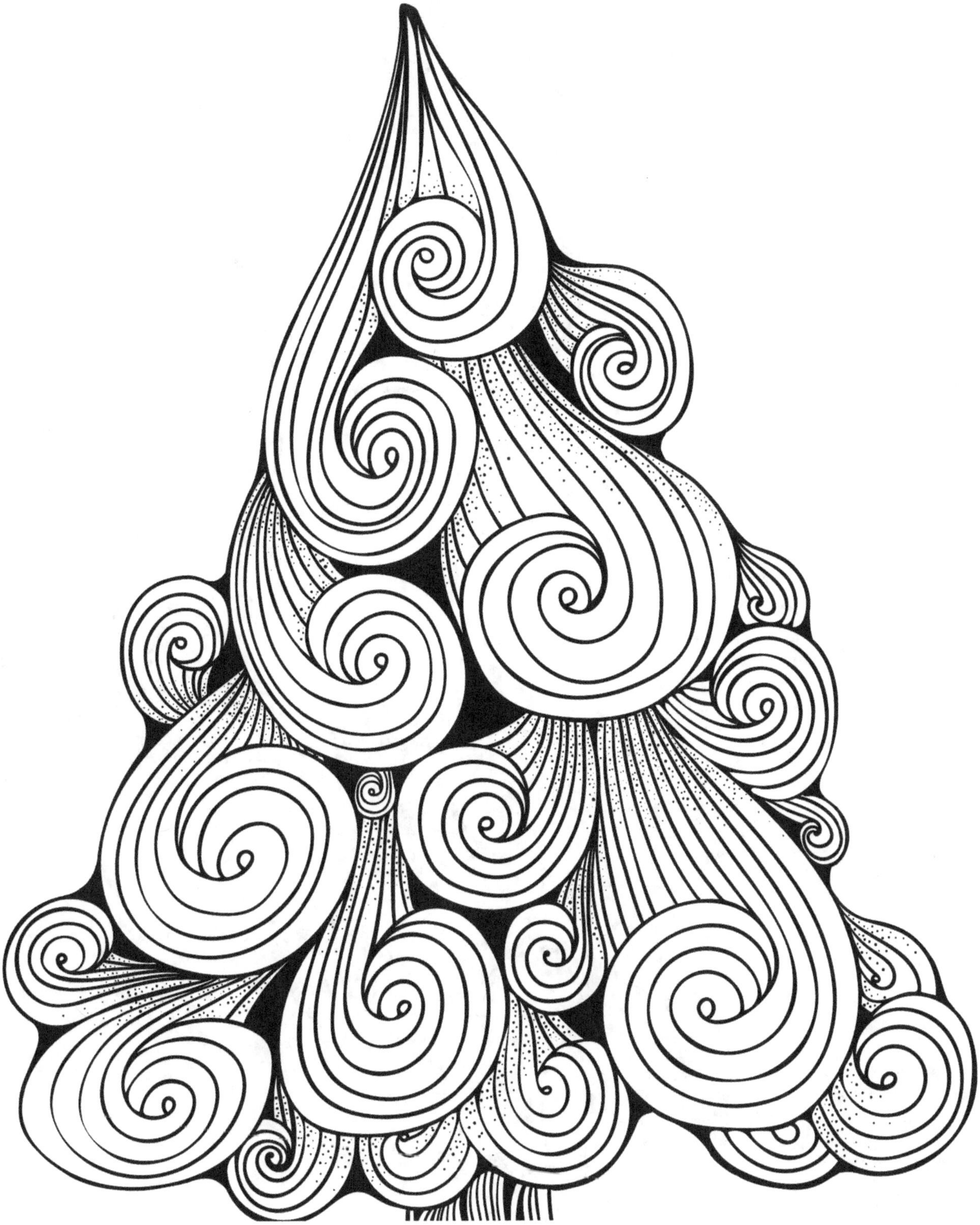

UH OH, THIS RAINBOW MIGHT COME WITH A LITTLE EXTRA SPARKLE.

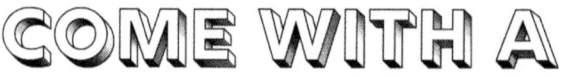

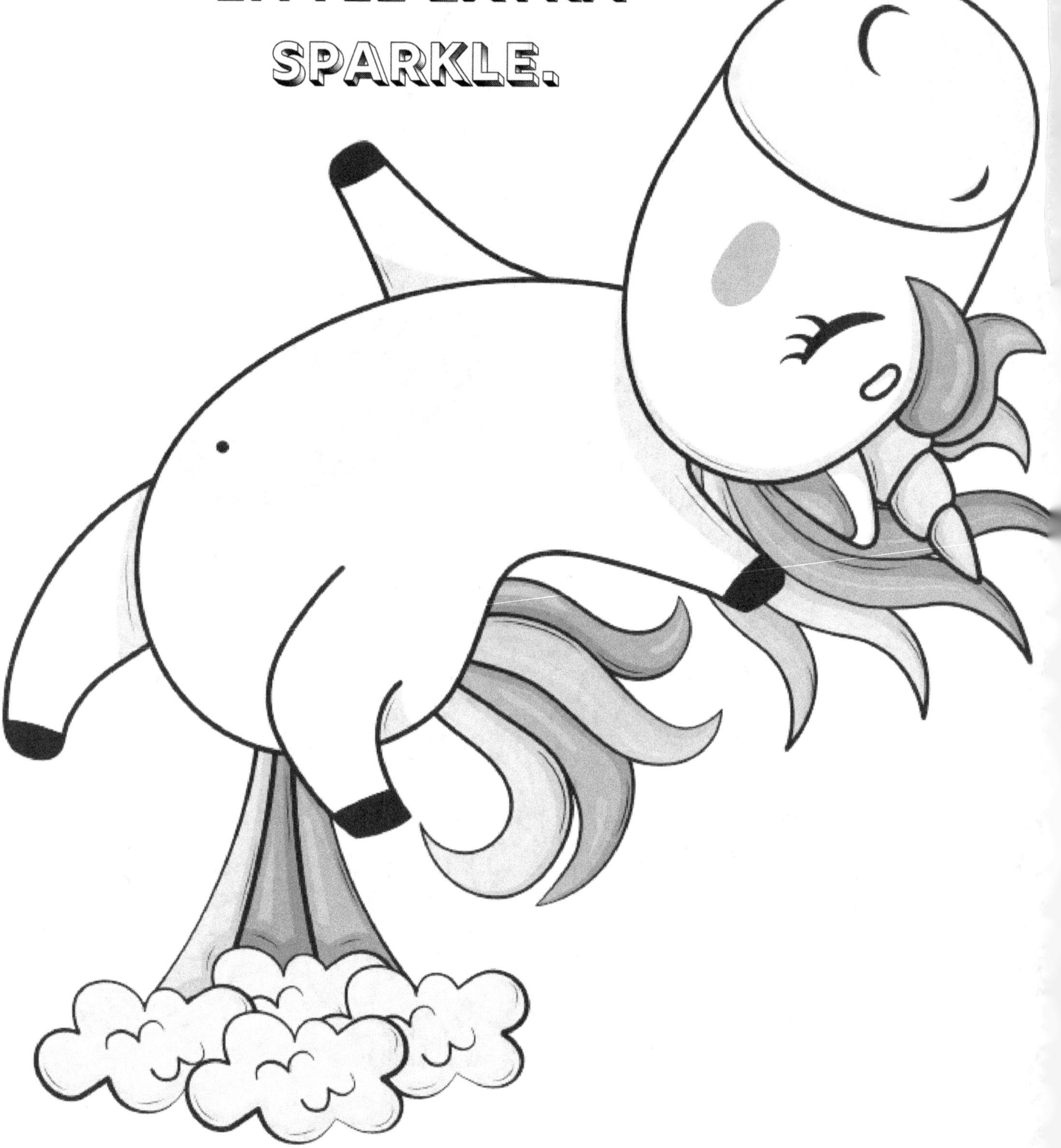

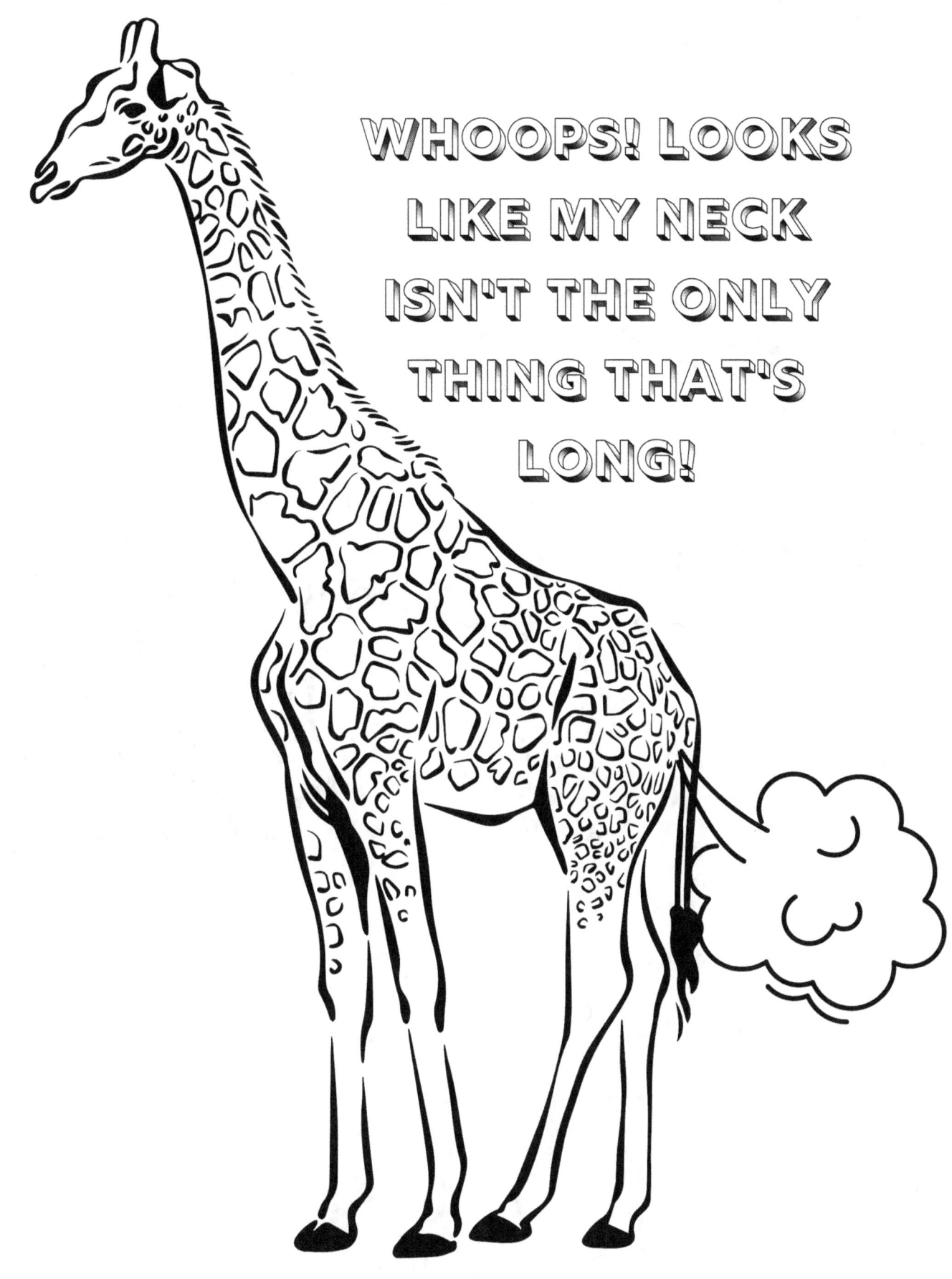

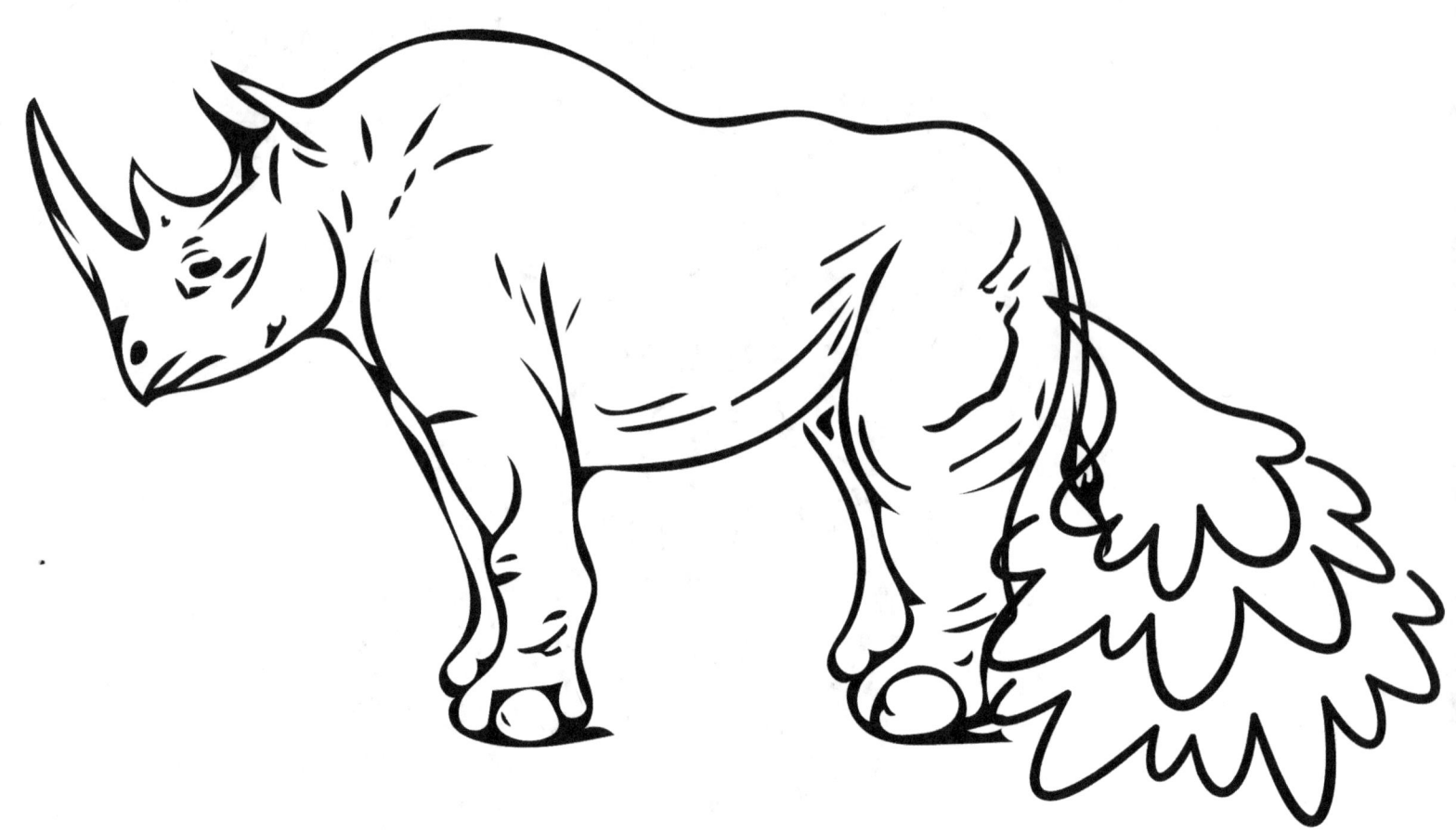

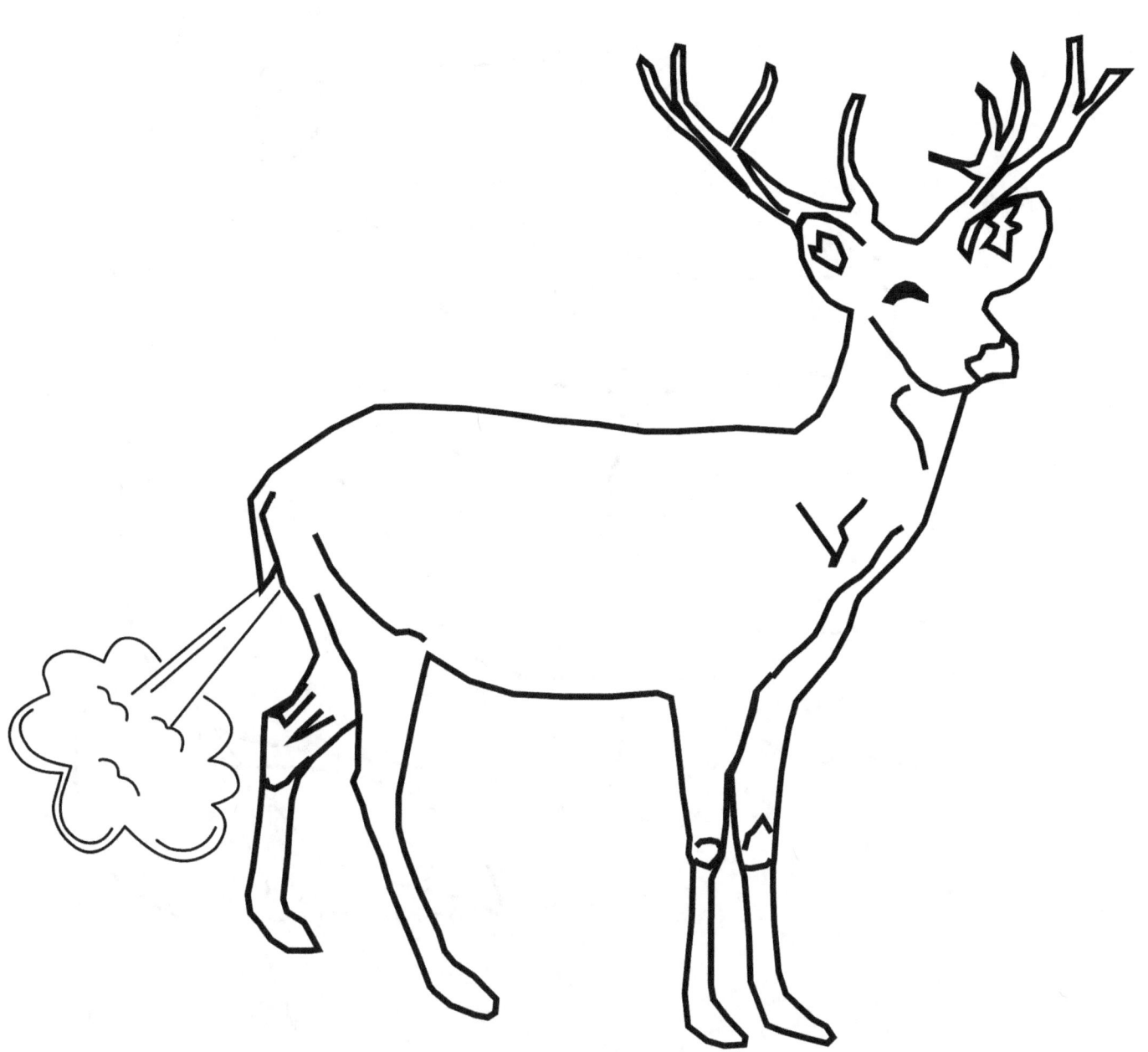

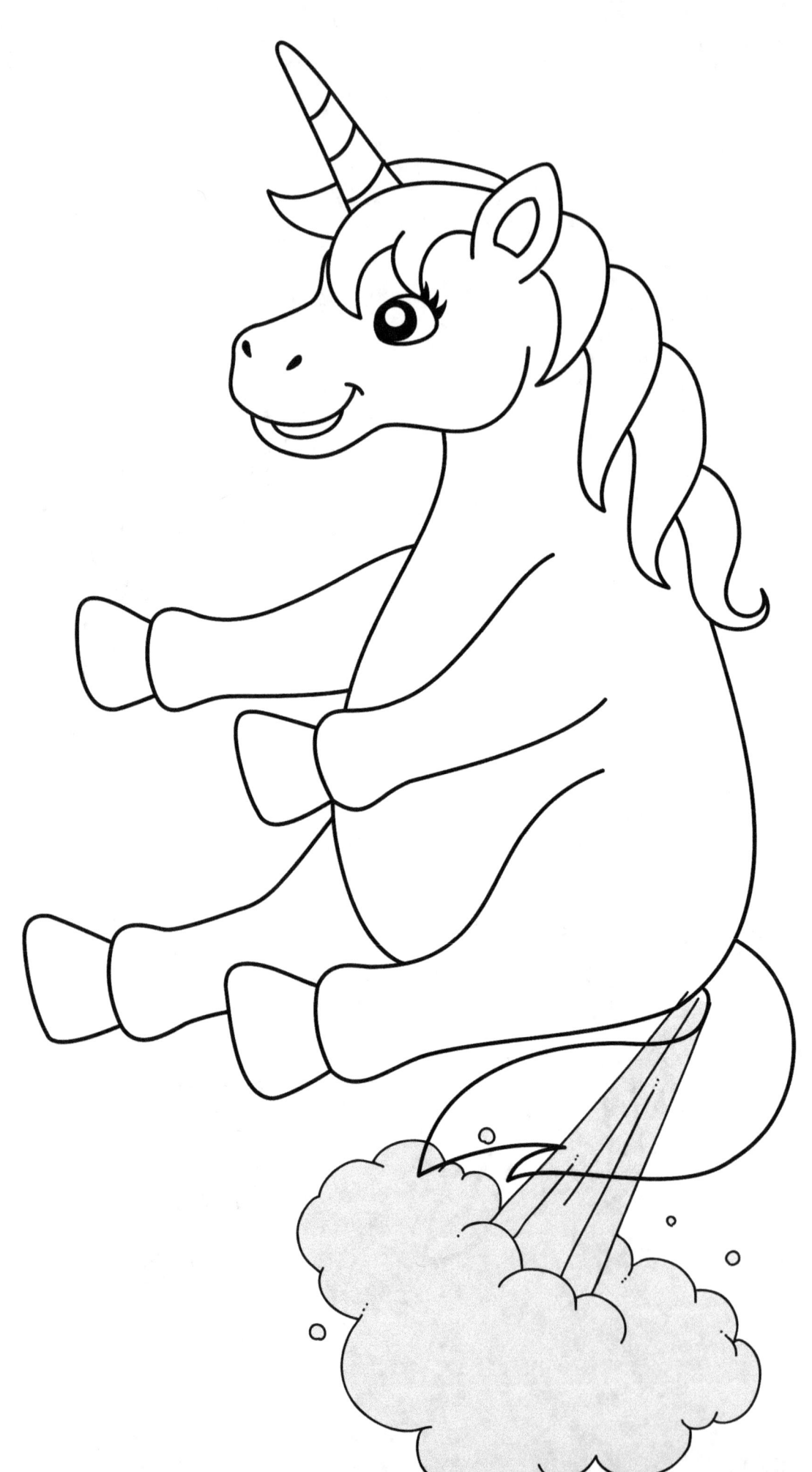

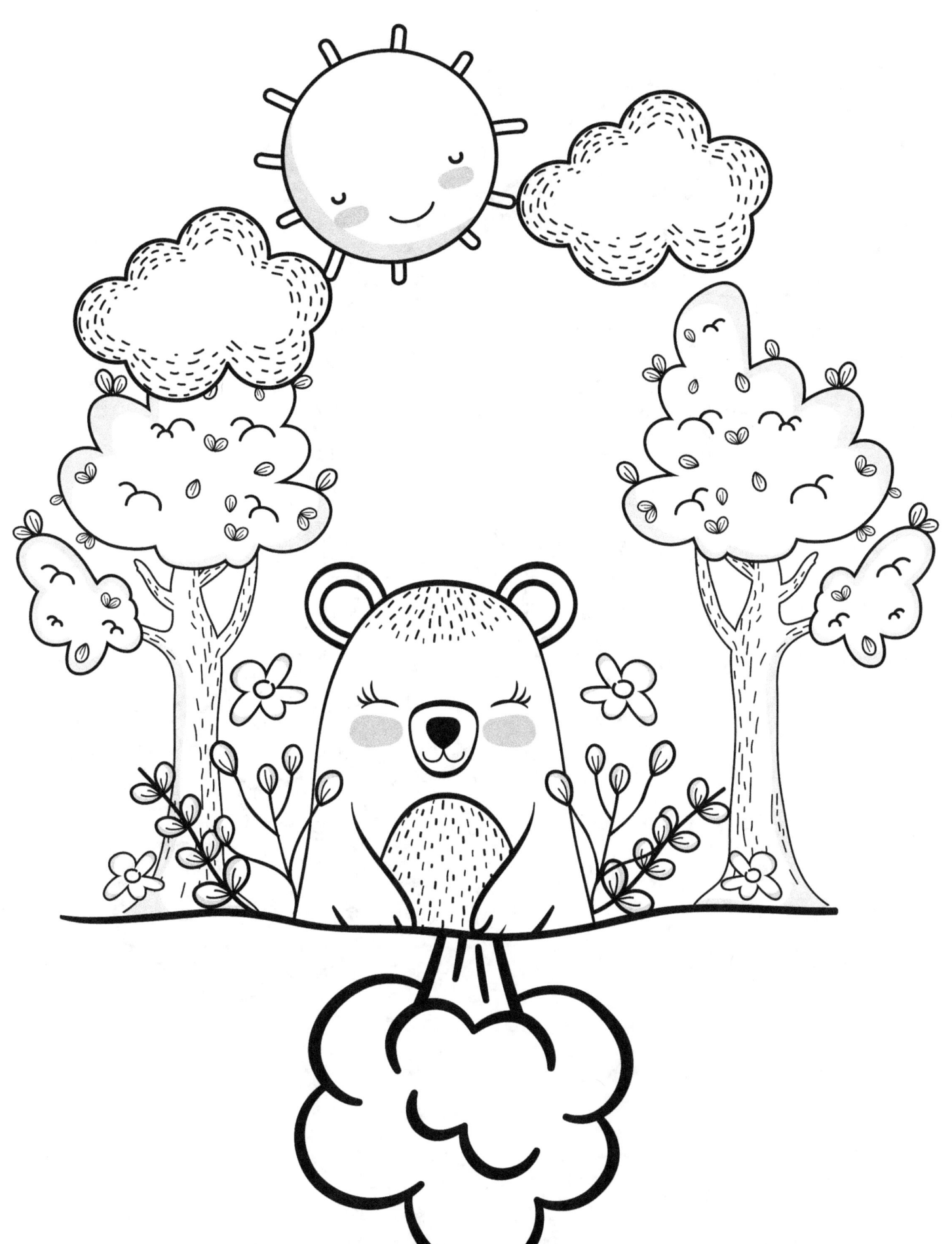

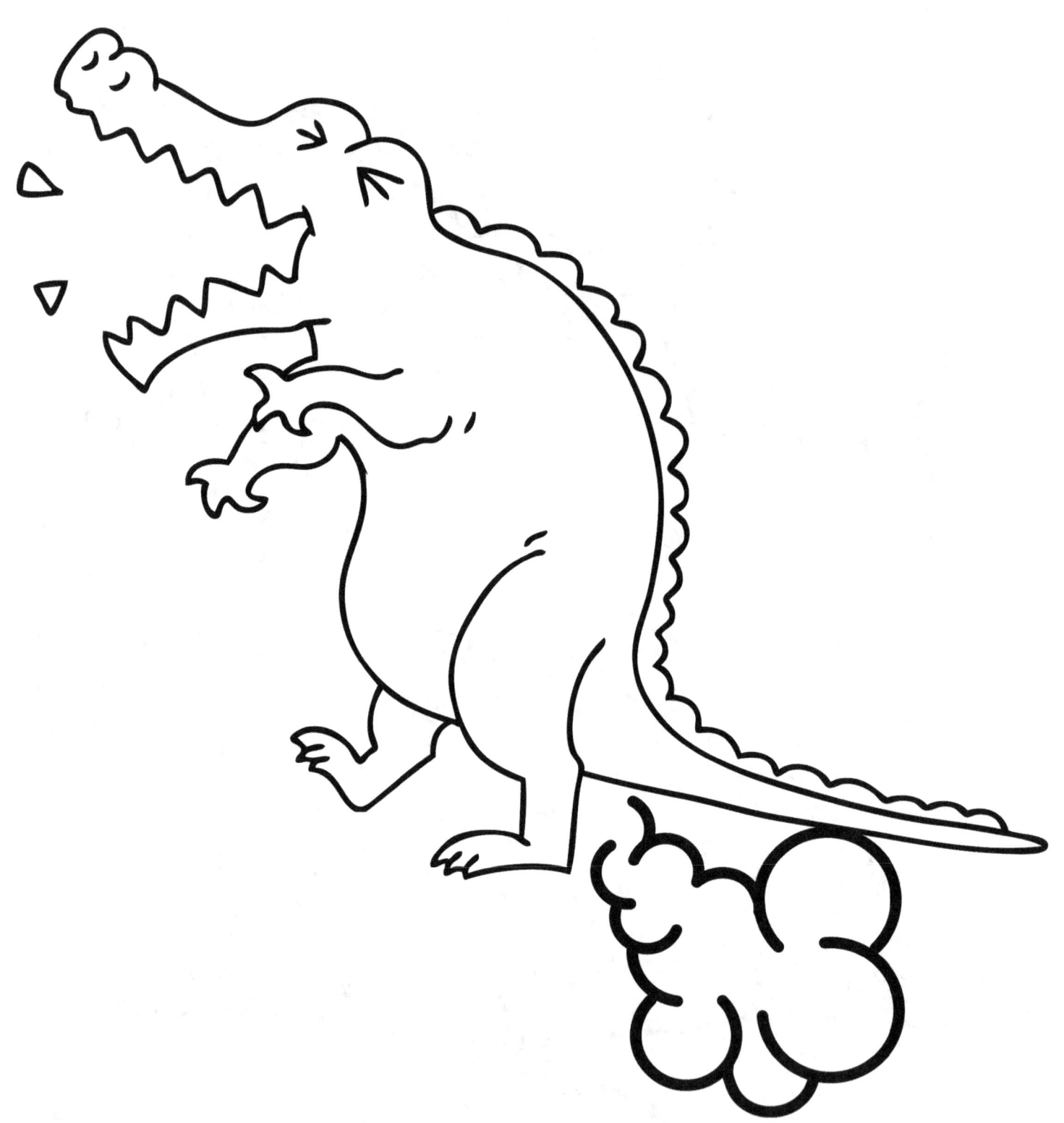

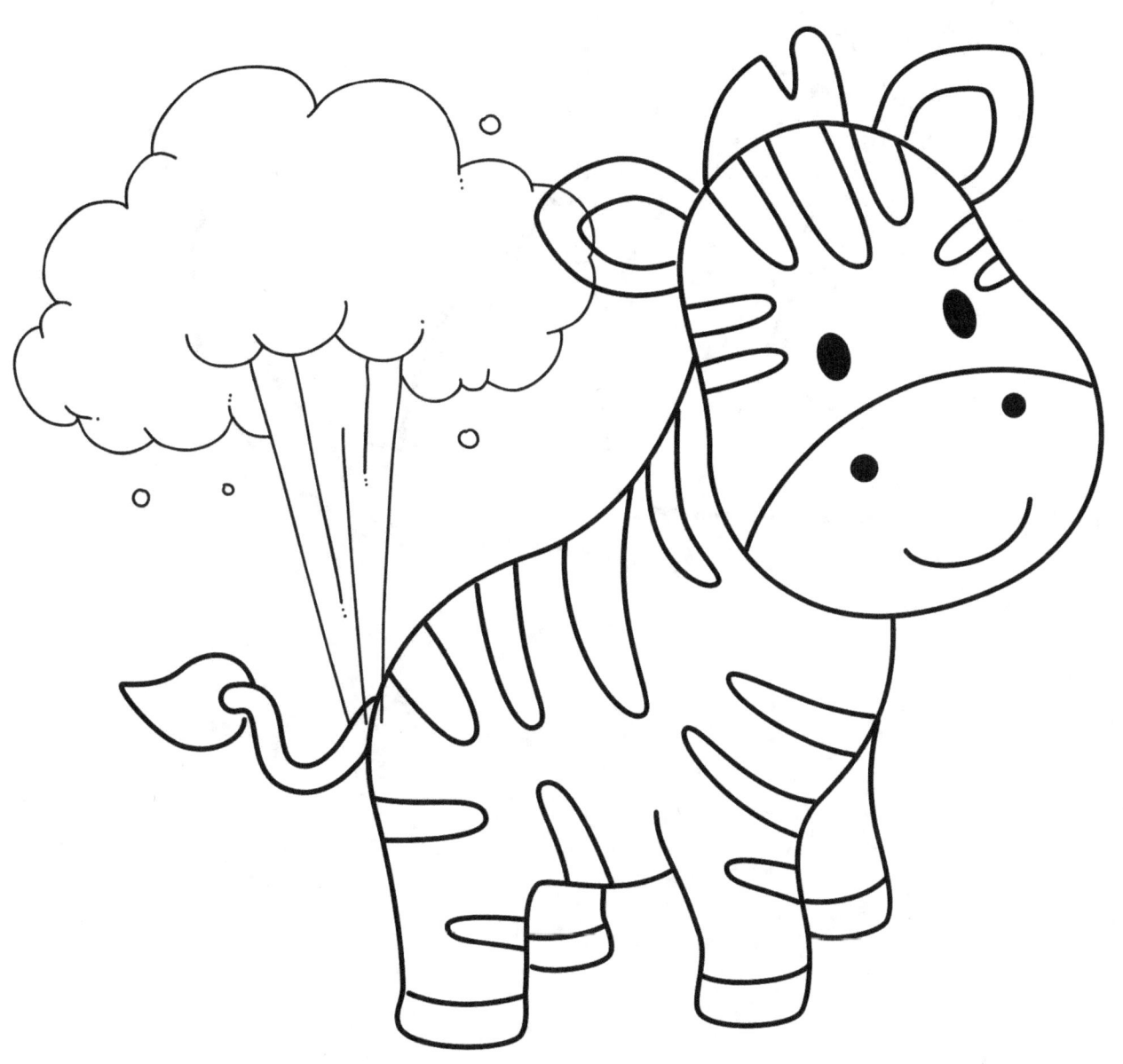

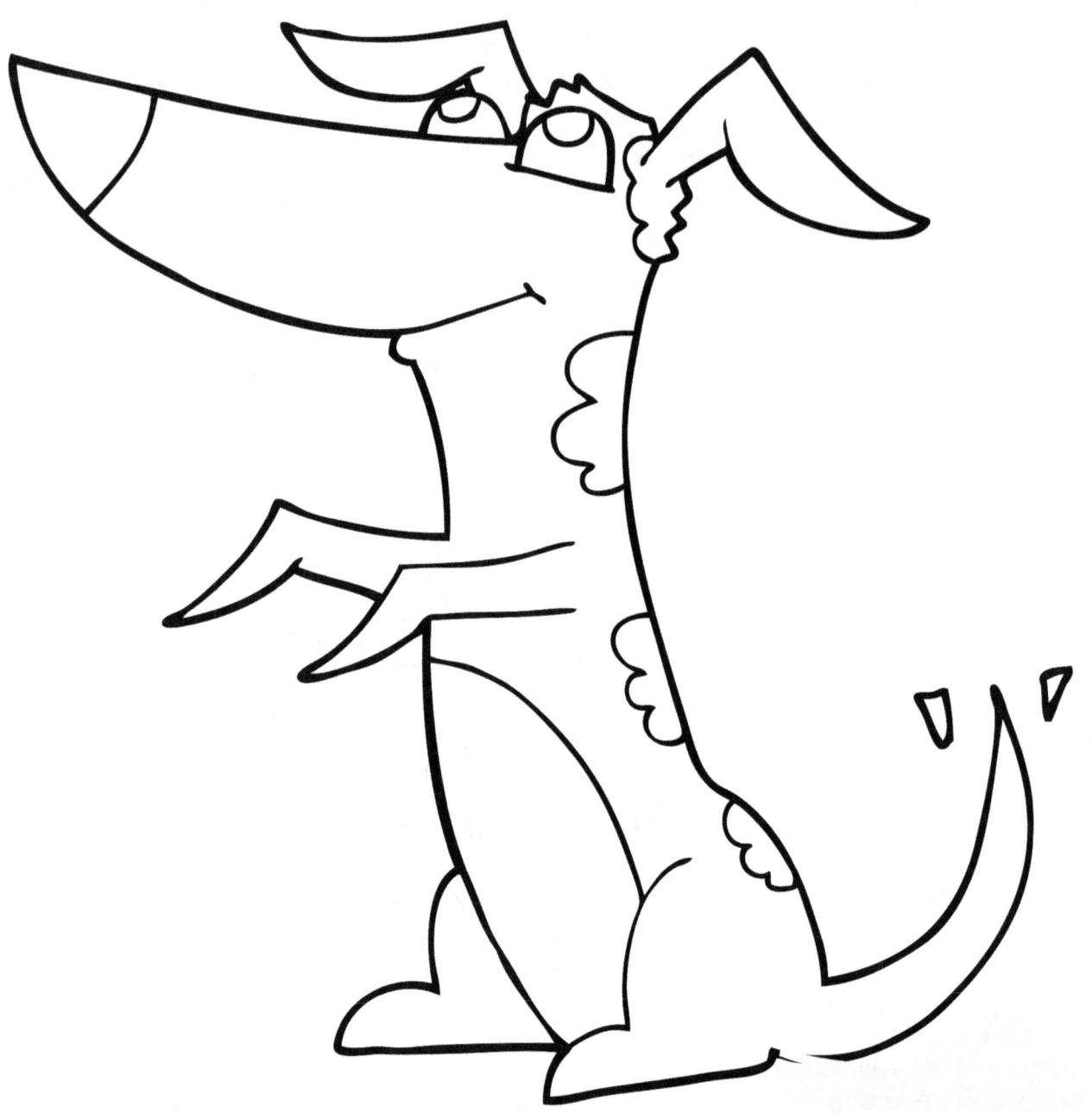

# MY HORN MAY BE MAGICAL, BUT APPARENTLY, SO IS MY TOOT

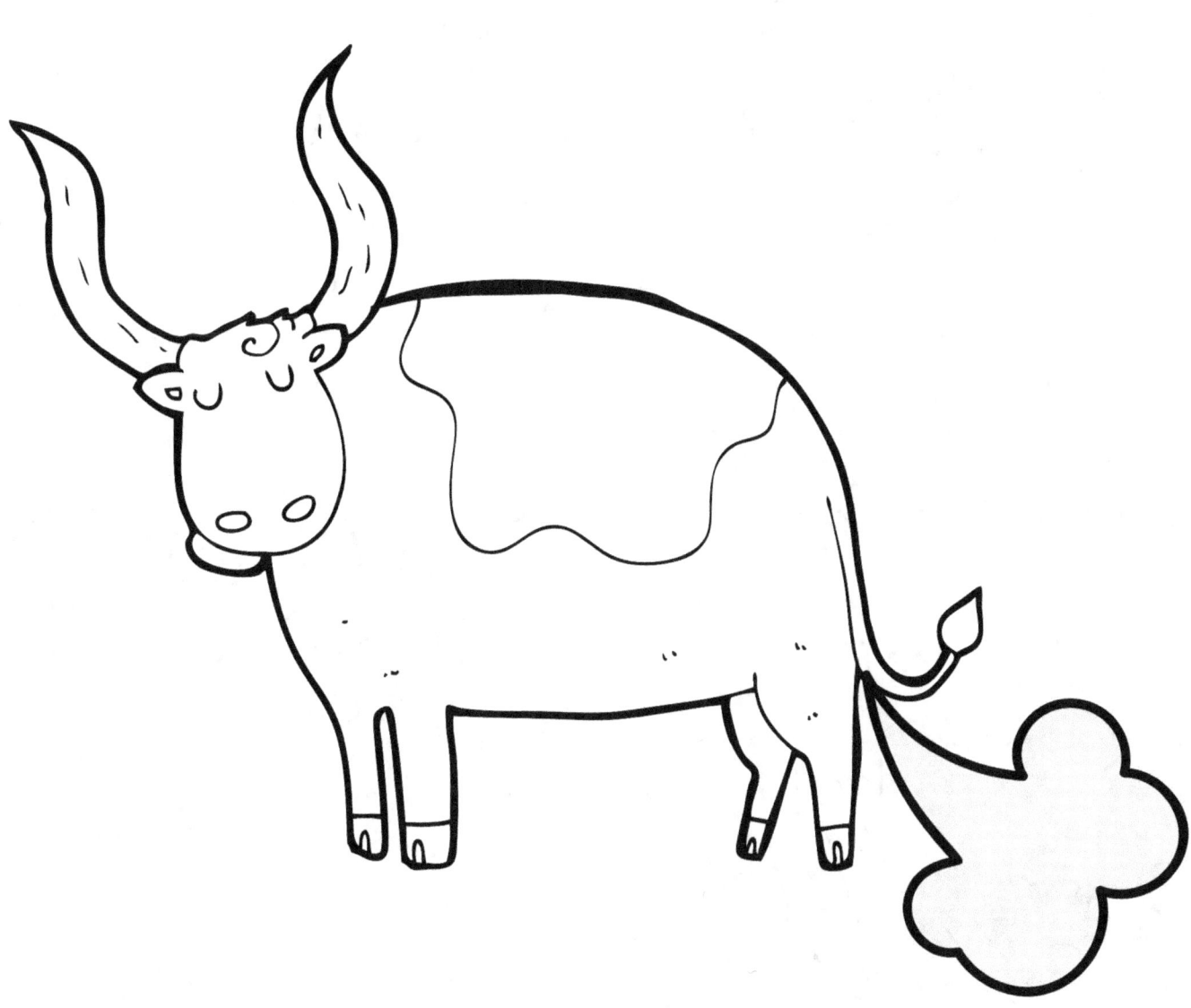

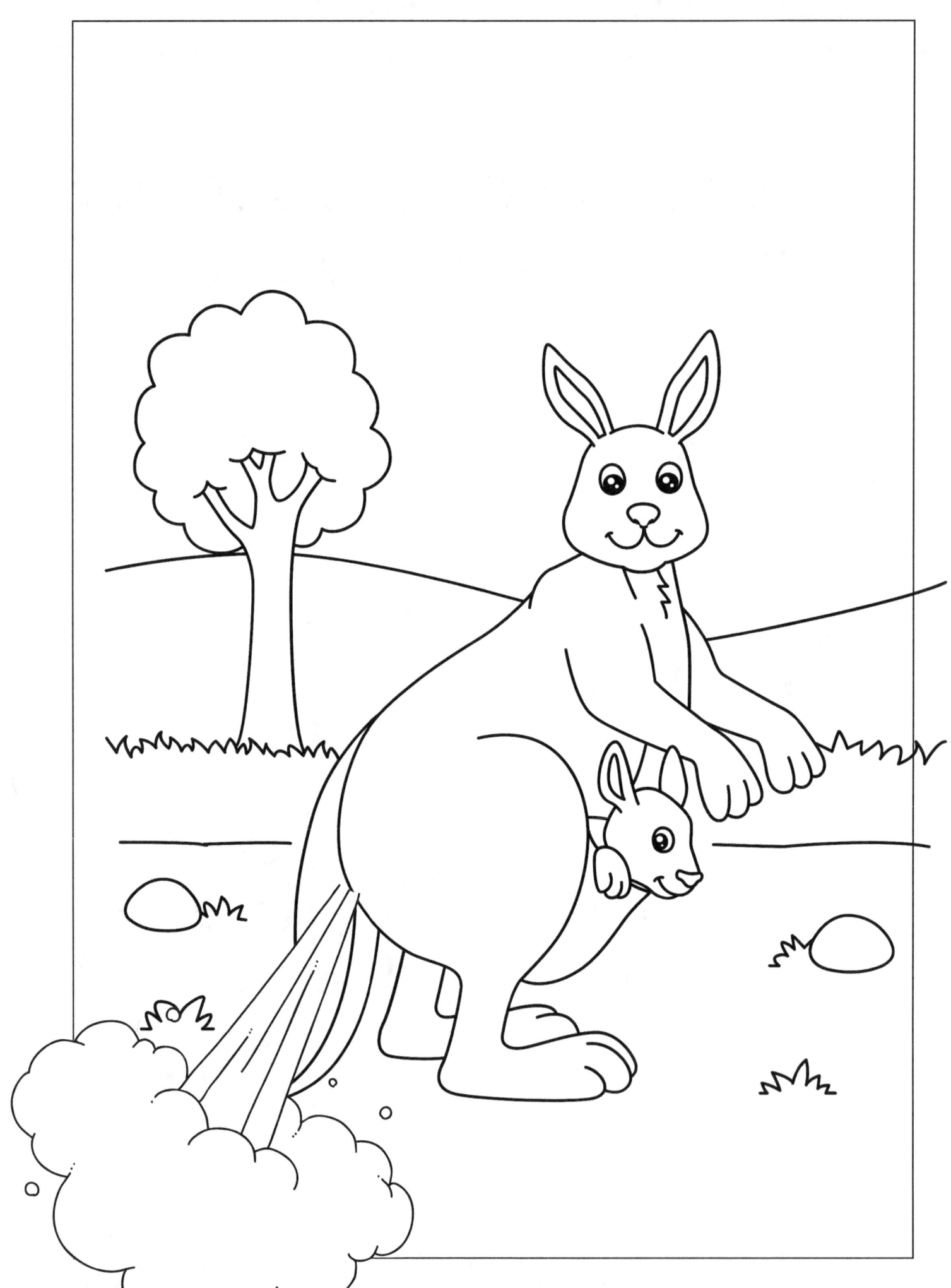

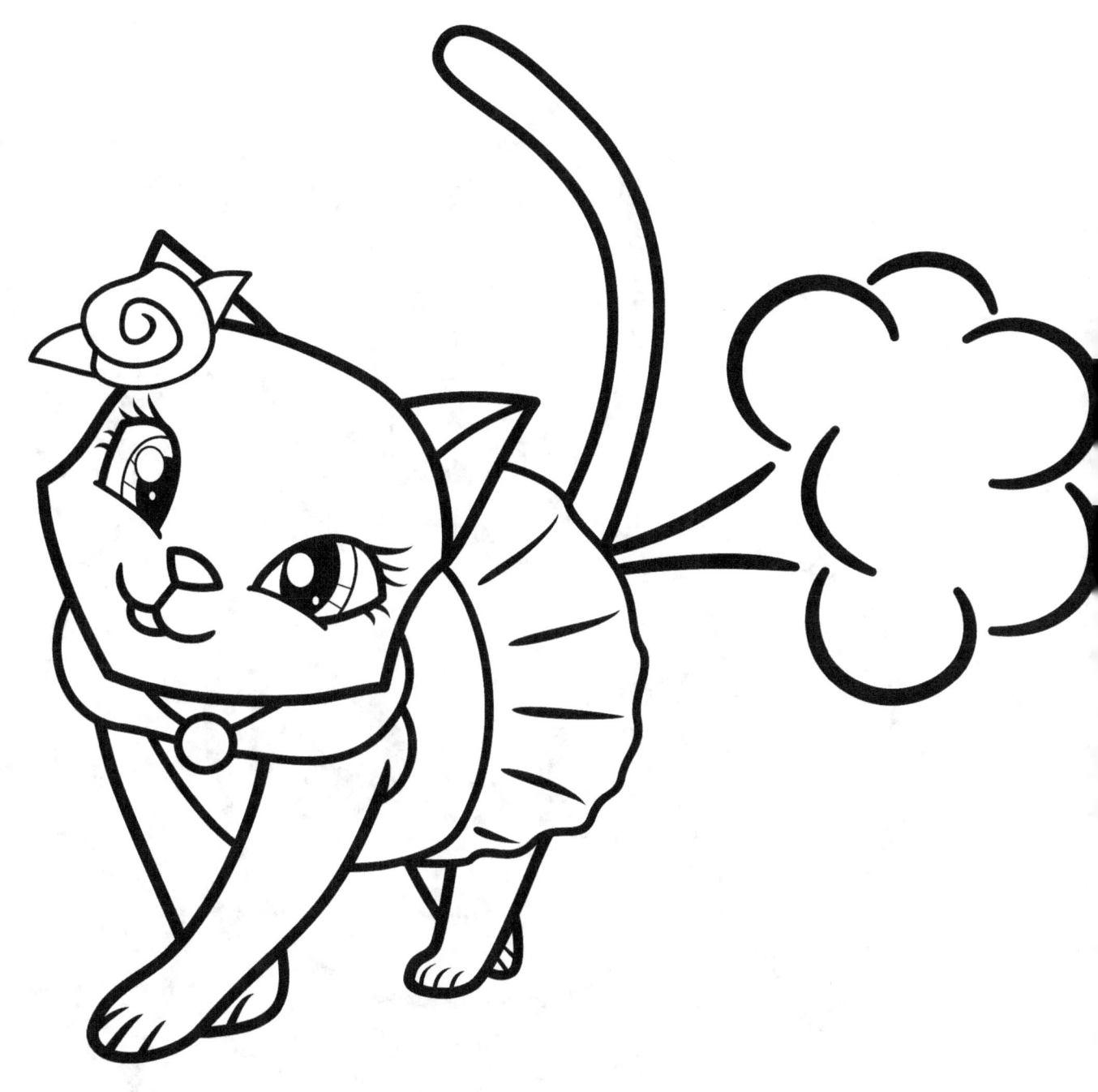

JUST DEODORIZING THE PREMISES. NOTHING TO SEE HERE, MEOW.

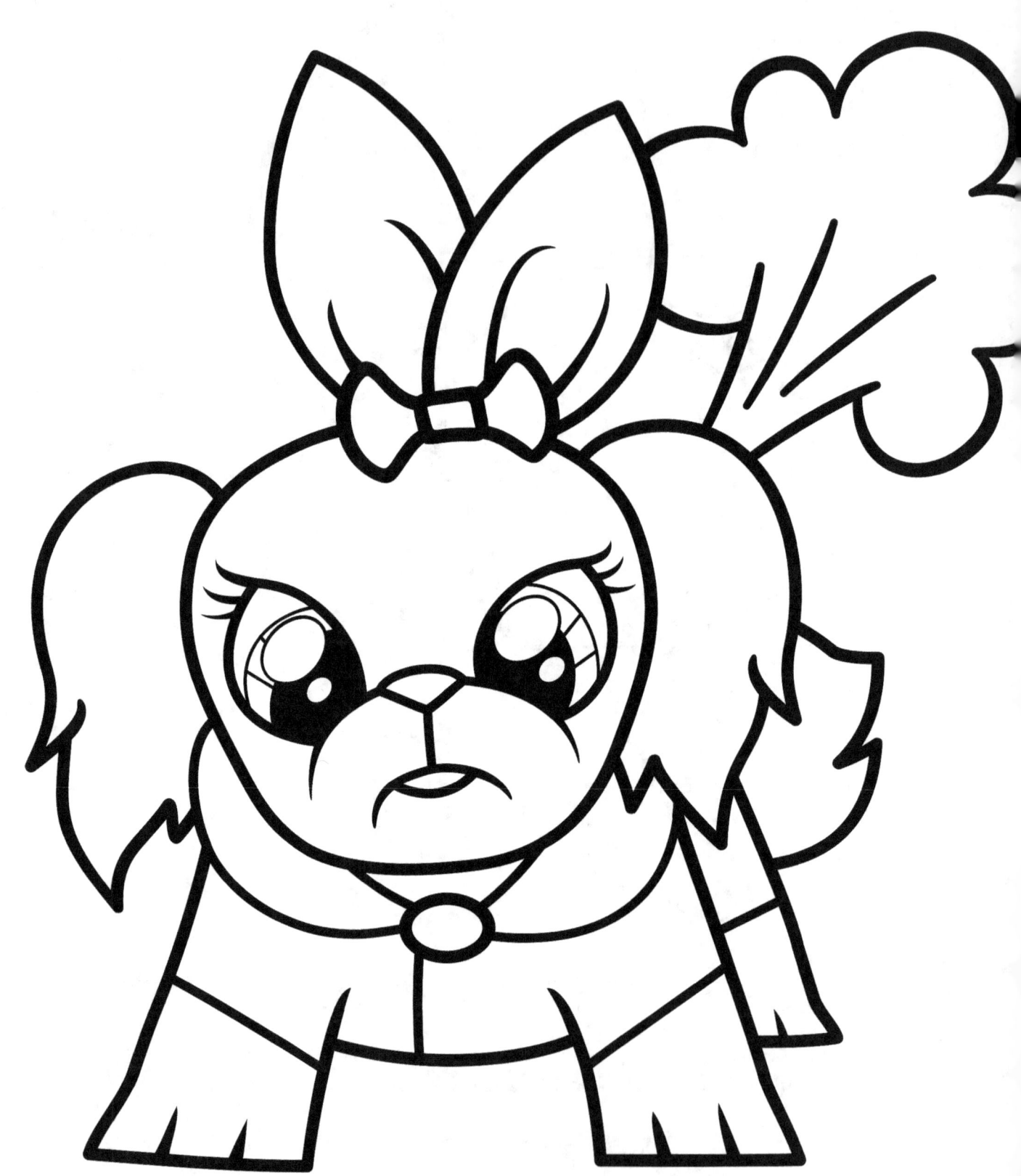

# OH, YOU WANTED TO CUDDLE? MAYBE LATER...AFTER SOME SERIOUS AIR FRESHENER.

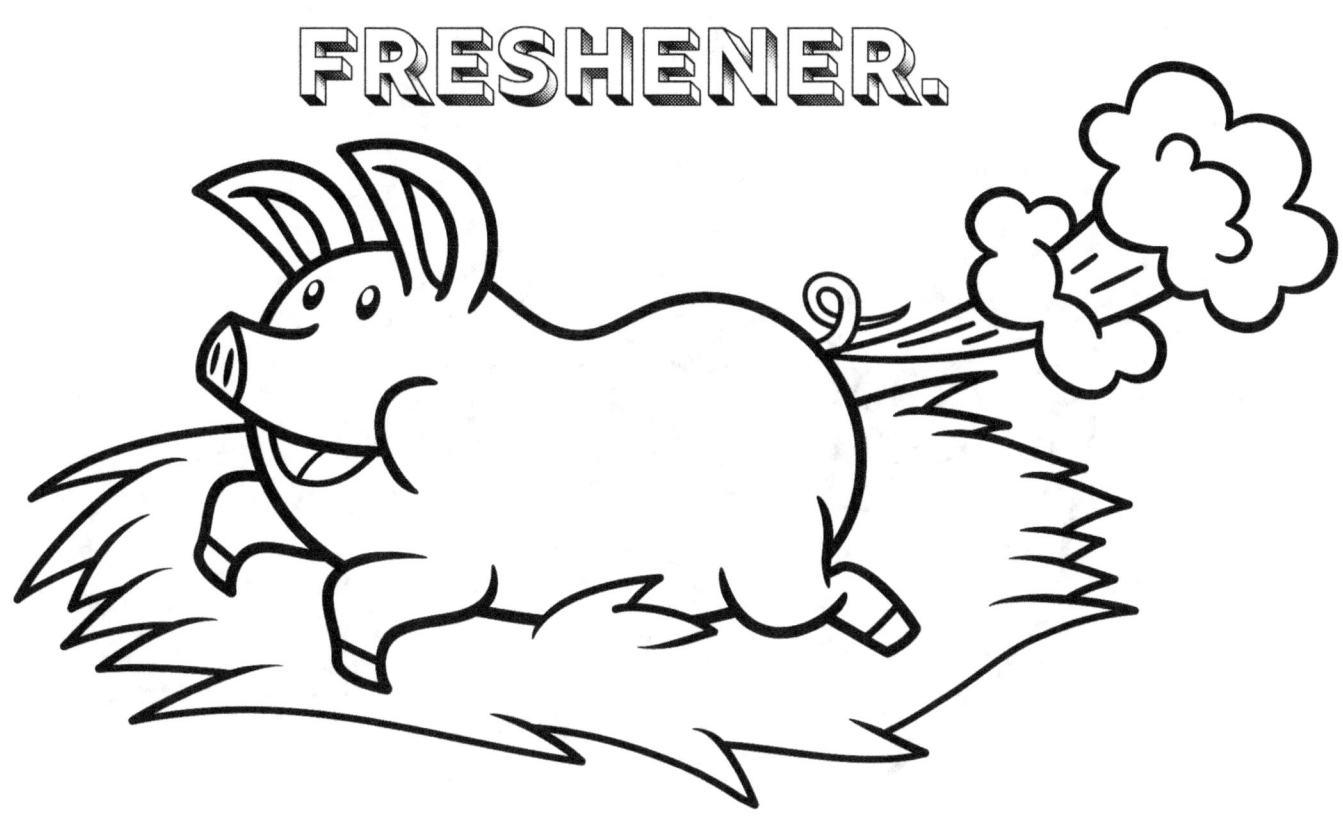

# MAYBE THOSE LEAVES WEREN'T AS HEALTHY AS I THOUGHT...

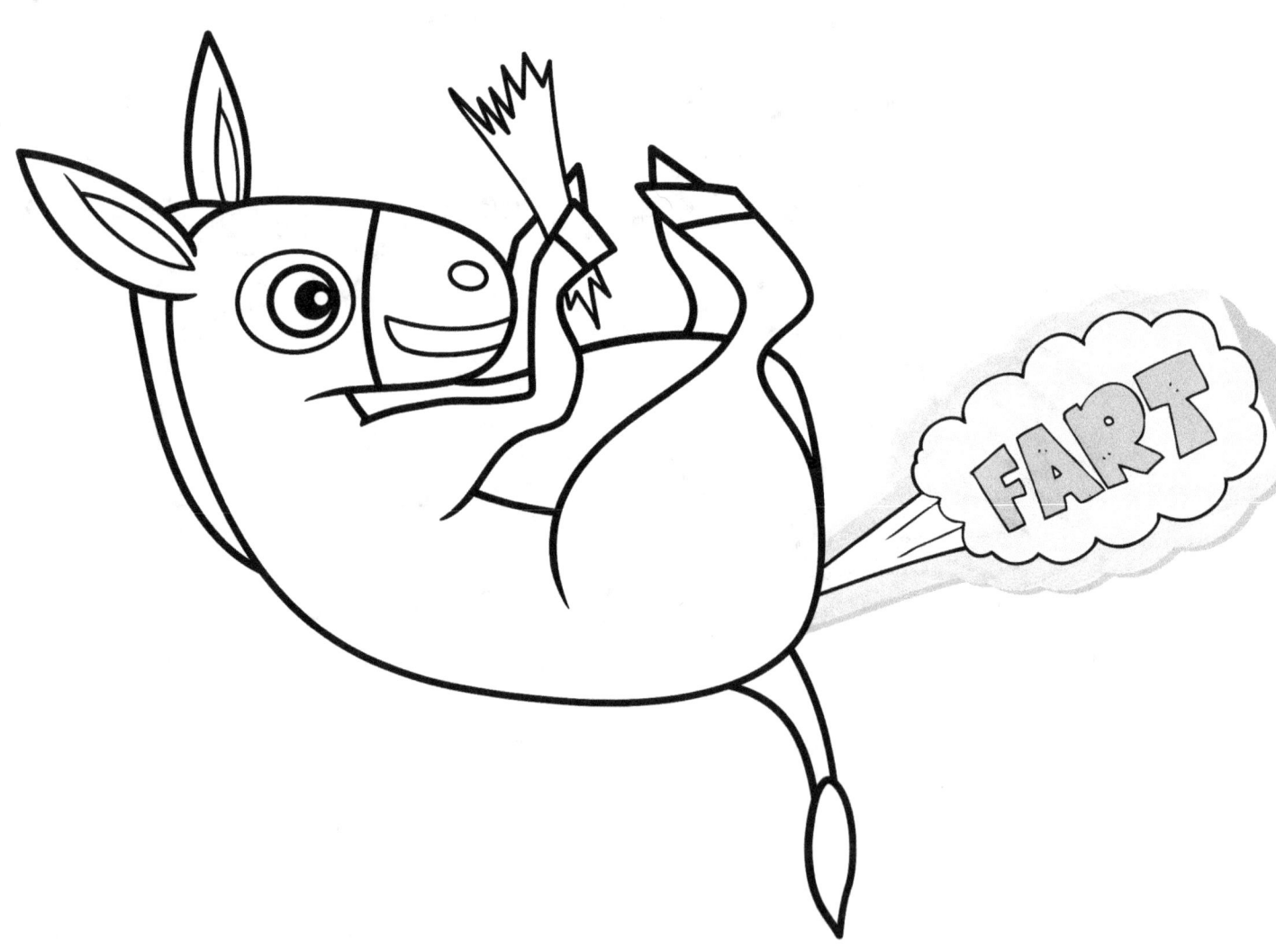

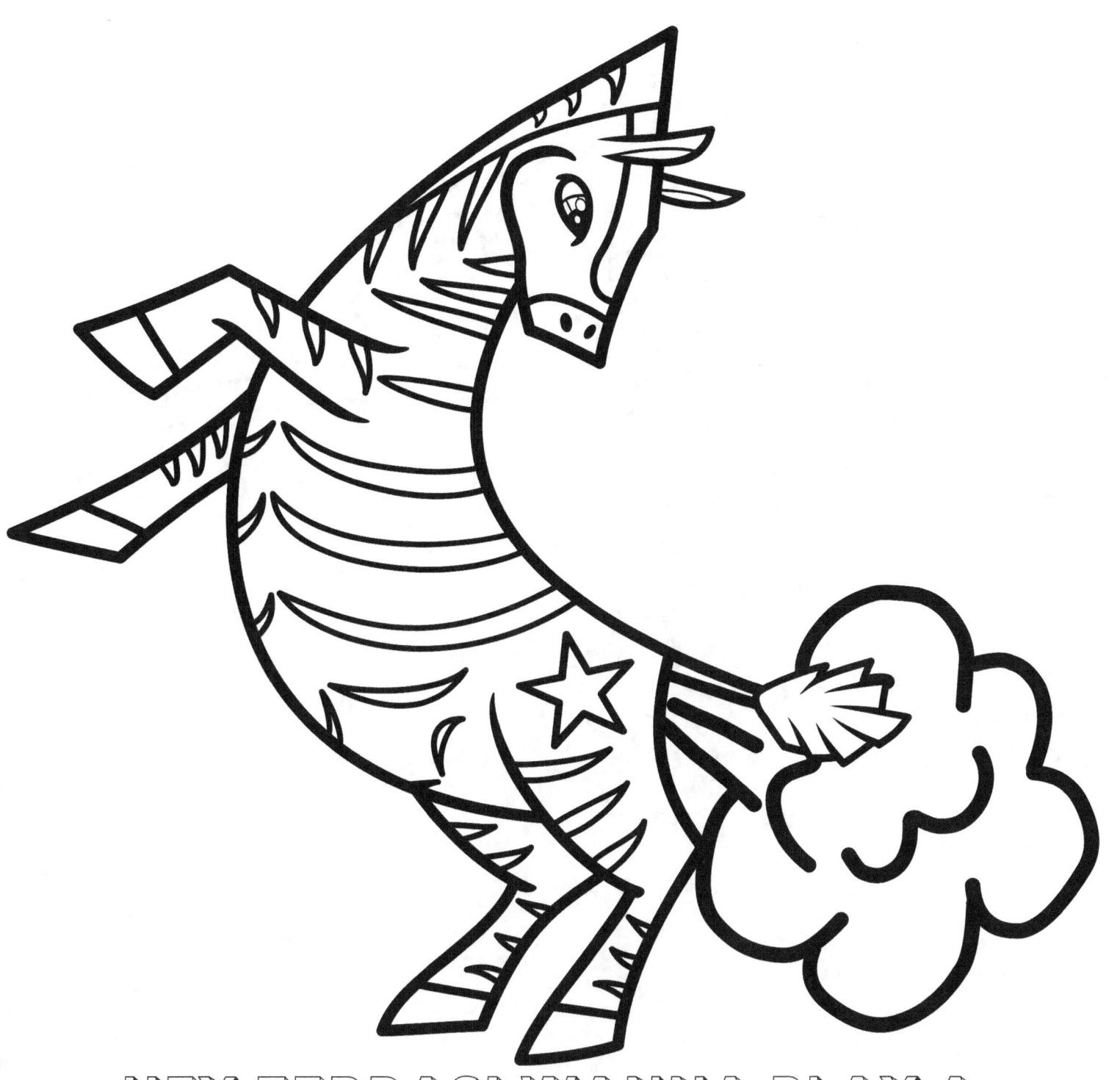

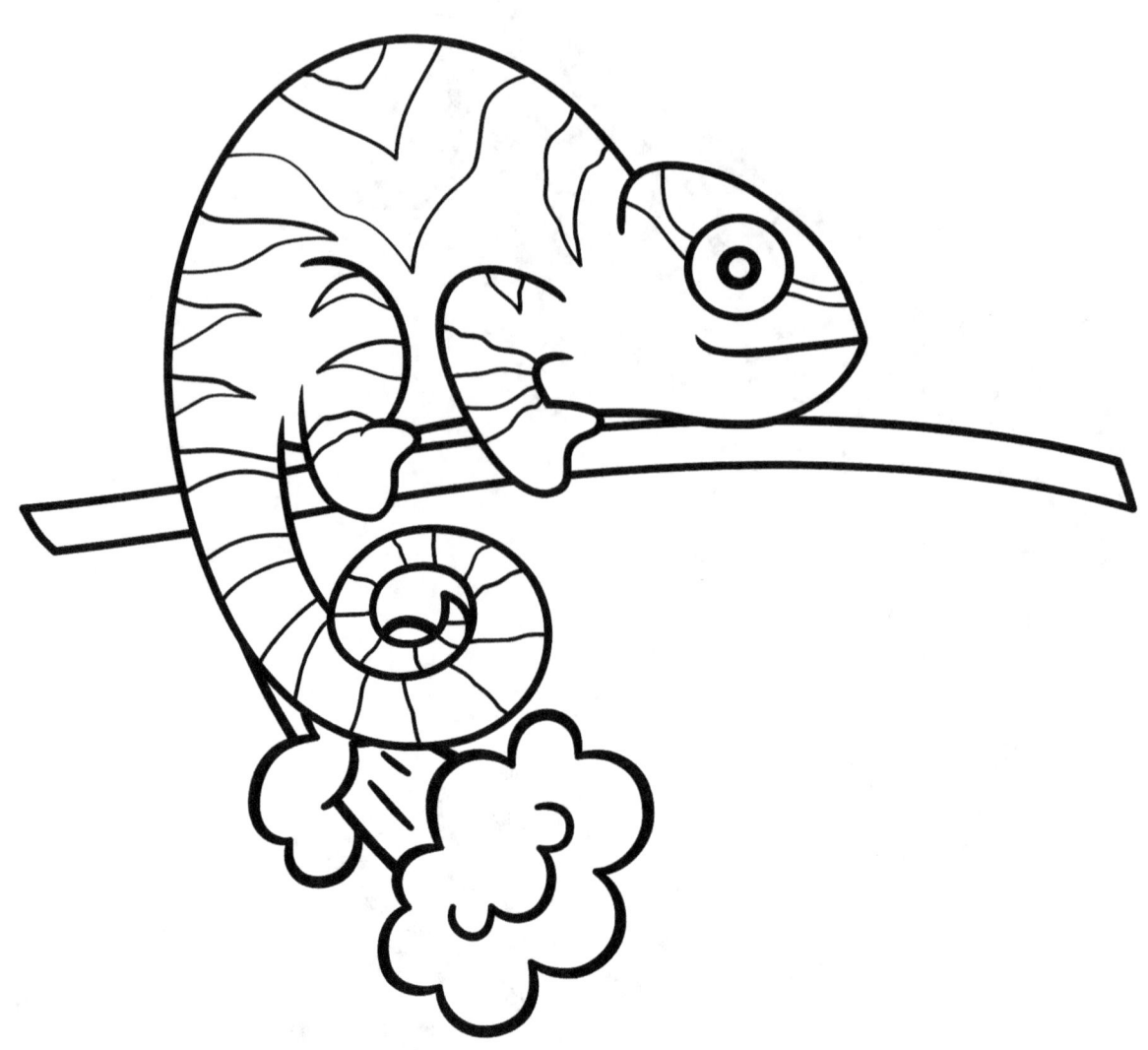

**MAYBE IF I COLOR THIS PAGE QUIETLY, NO ONE WILL NOTICE...**

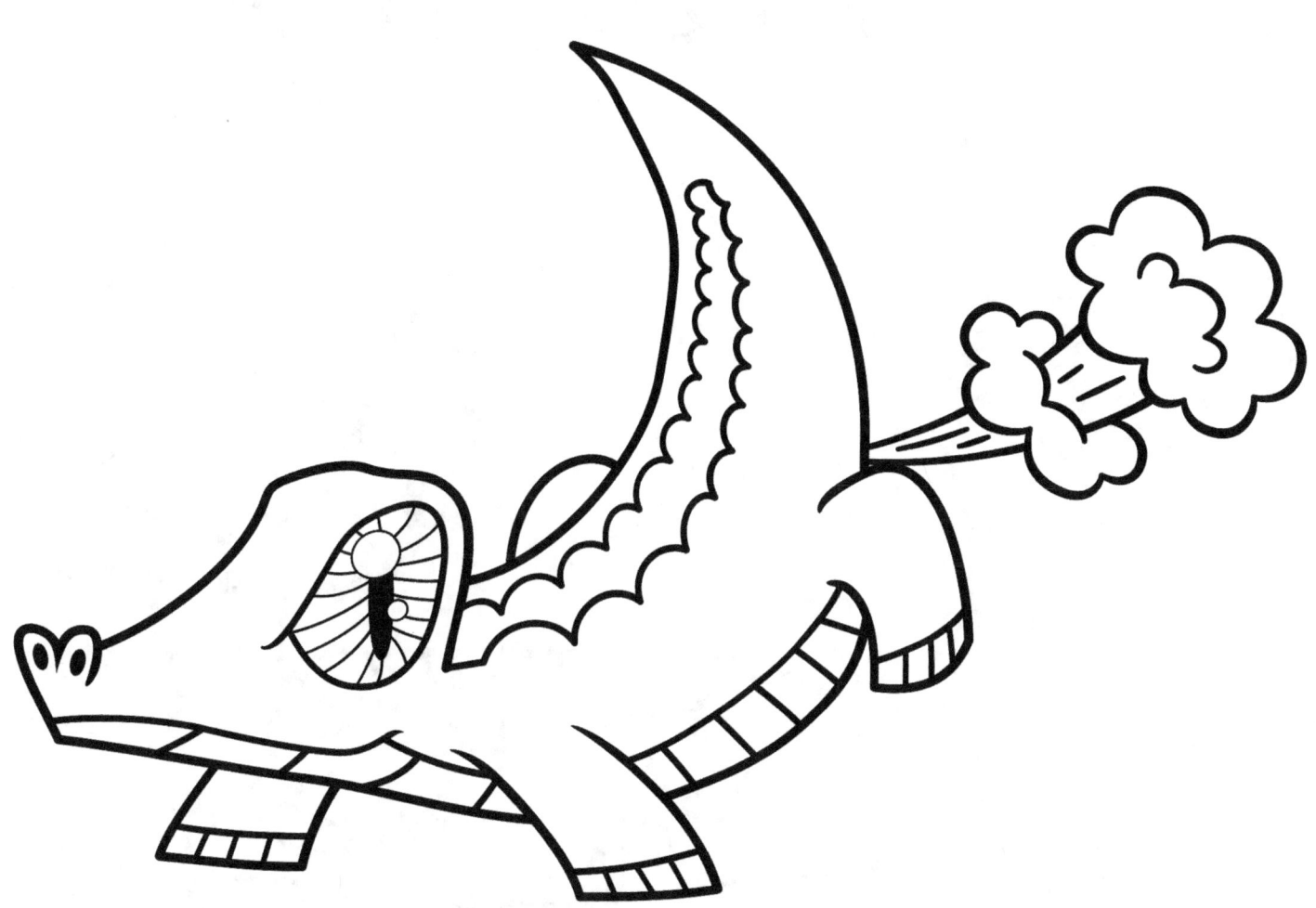

# I am the king so I fart more

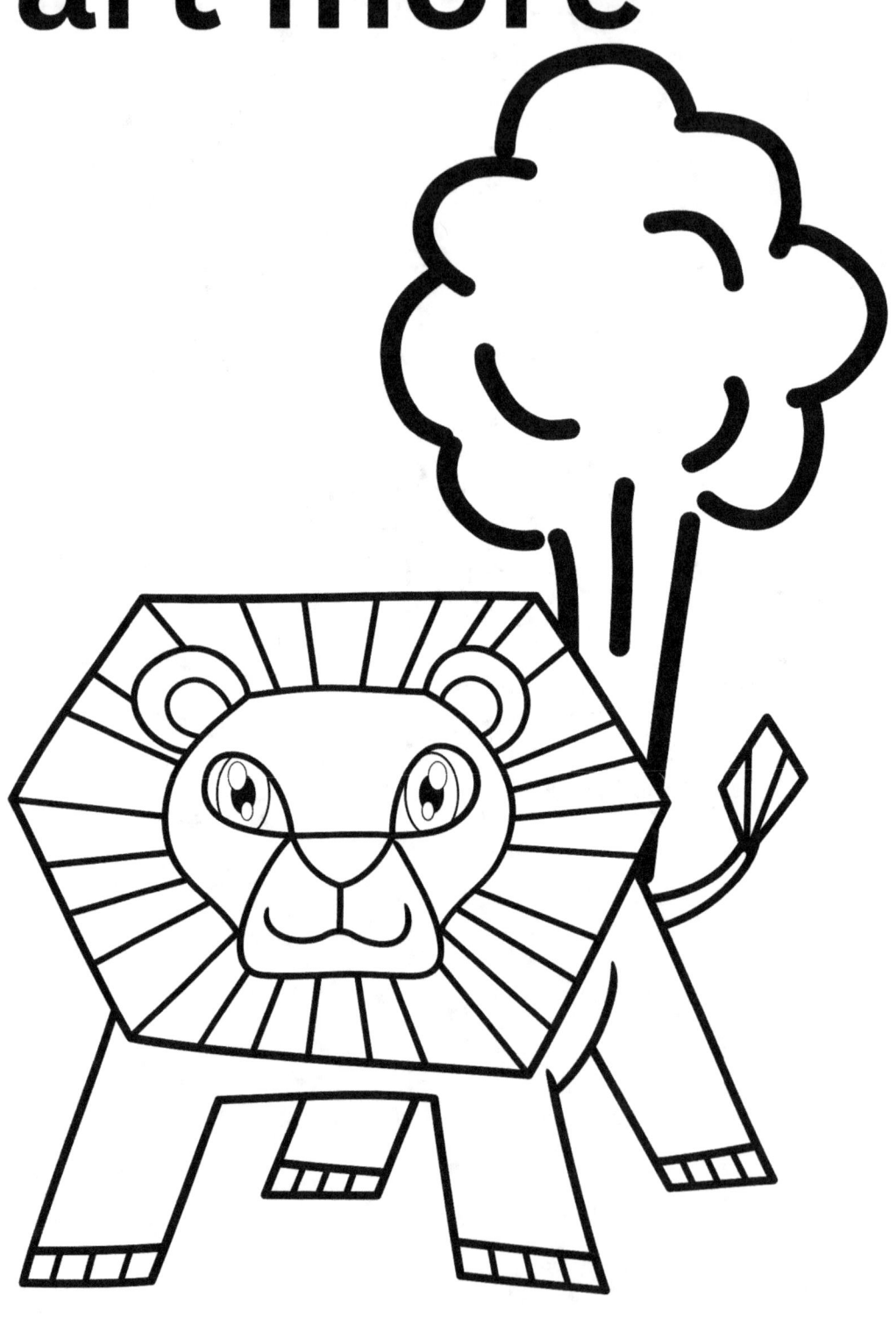

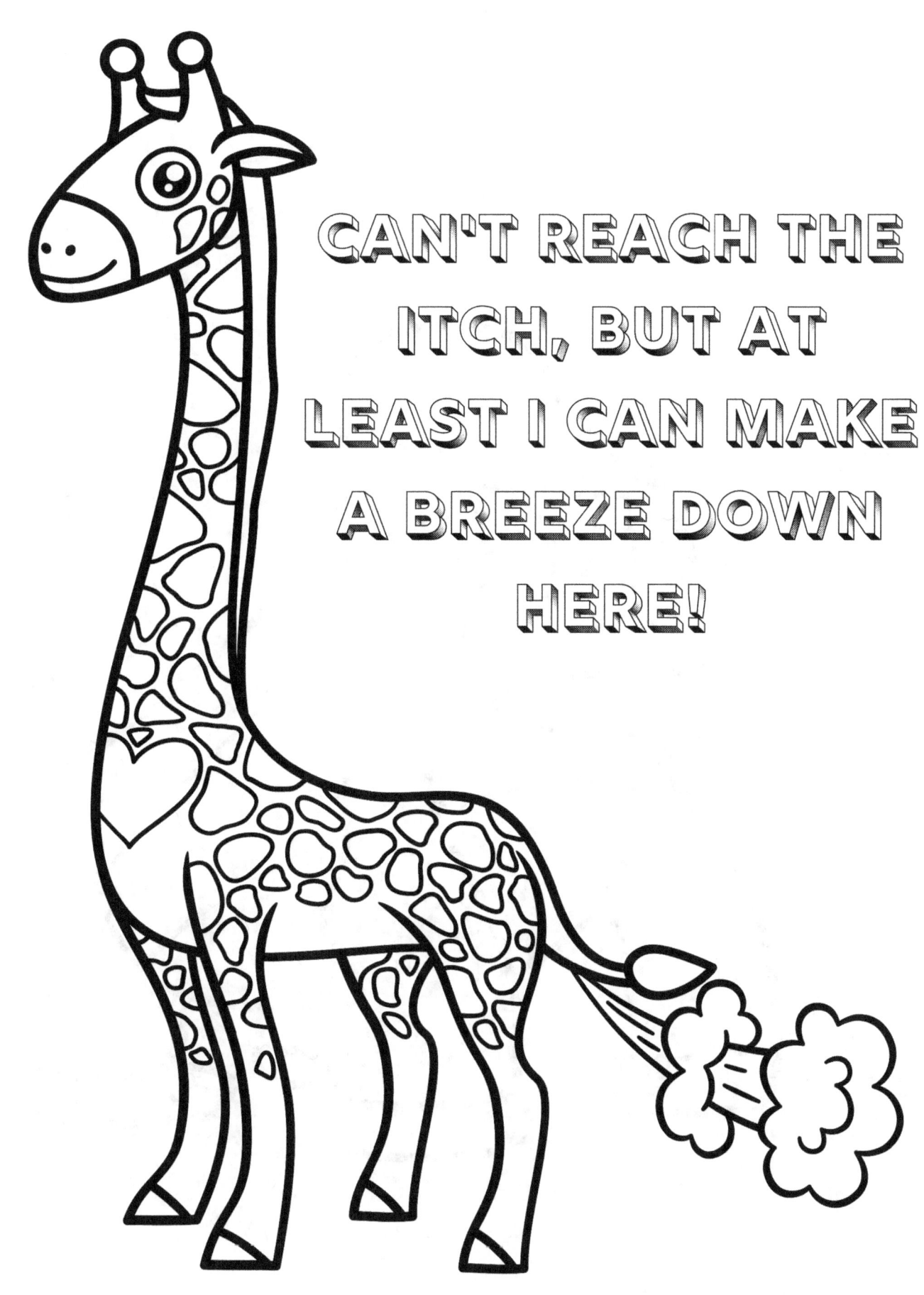

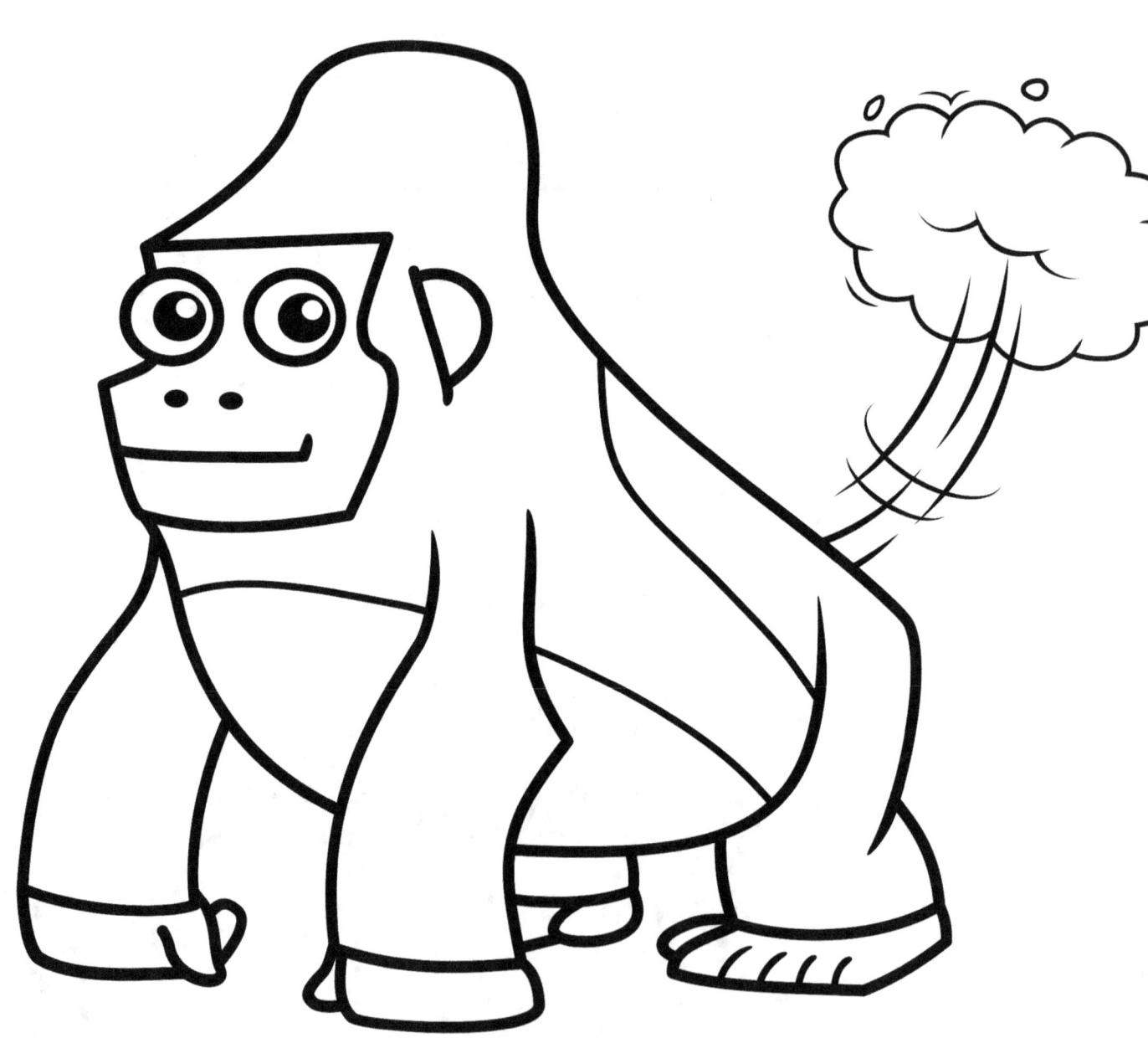

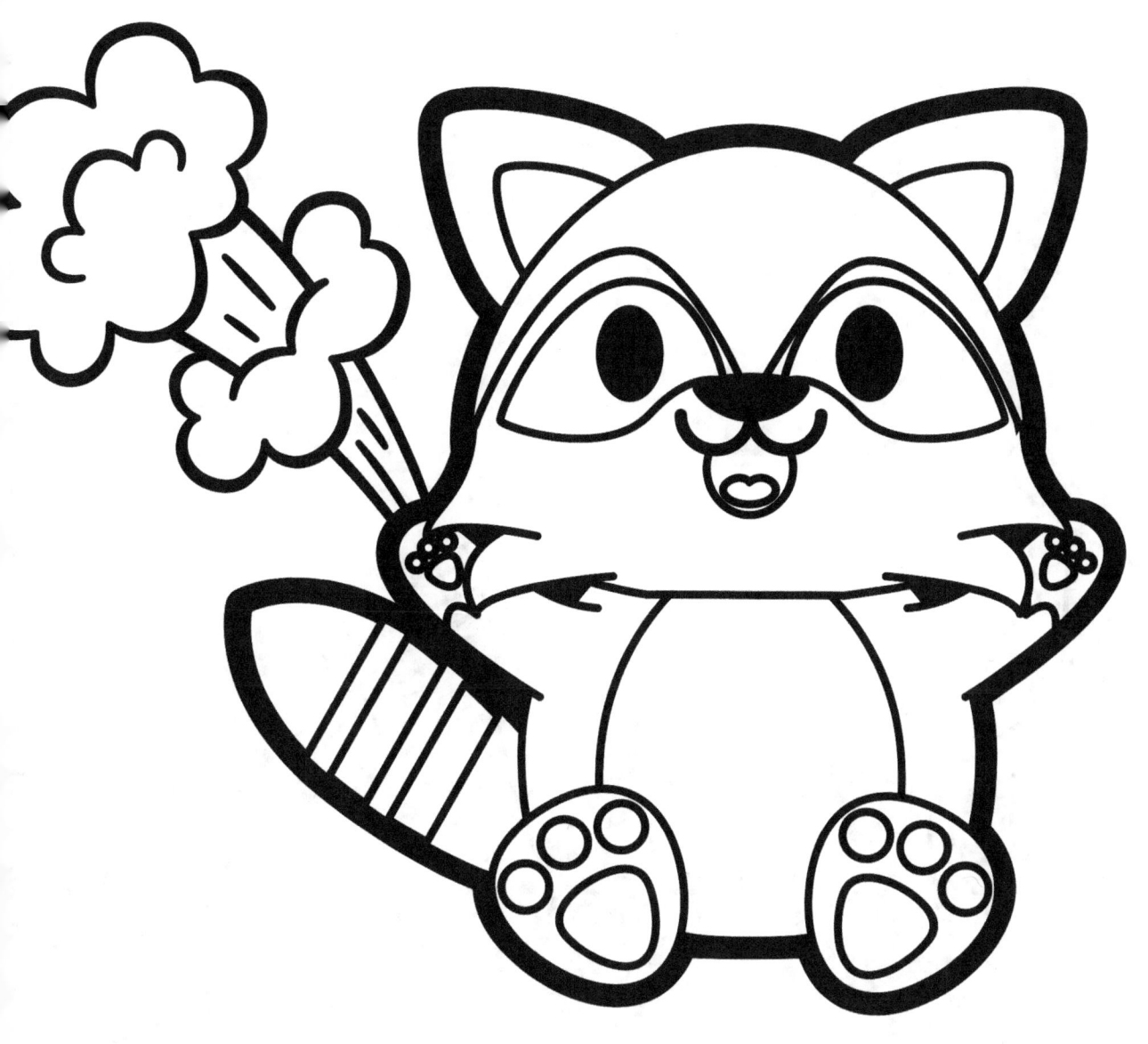

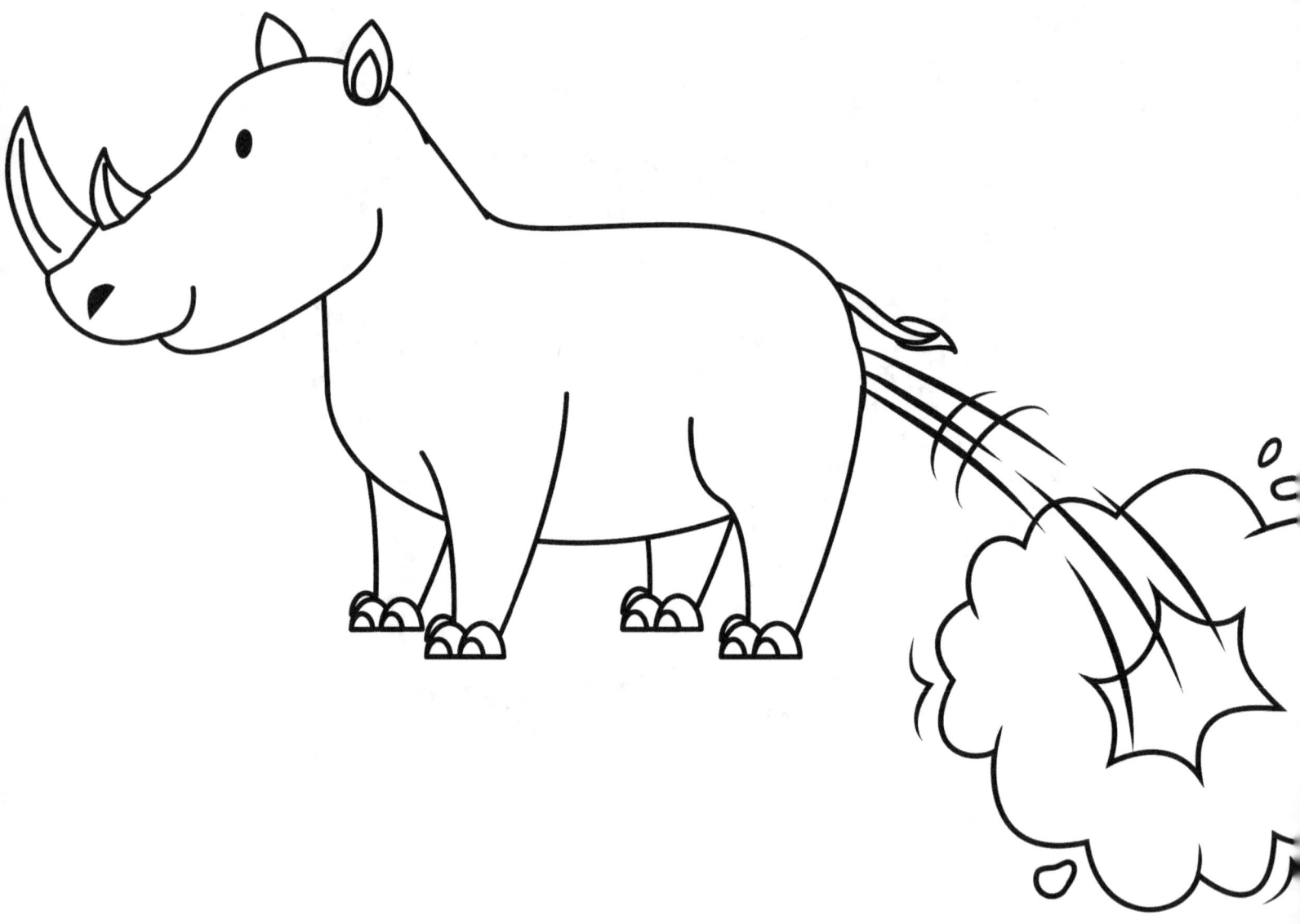

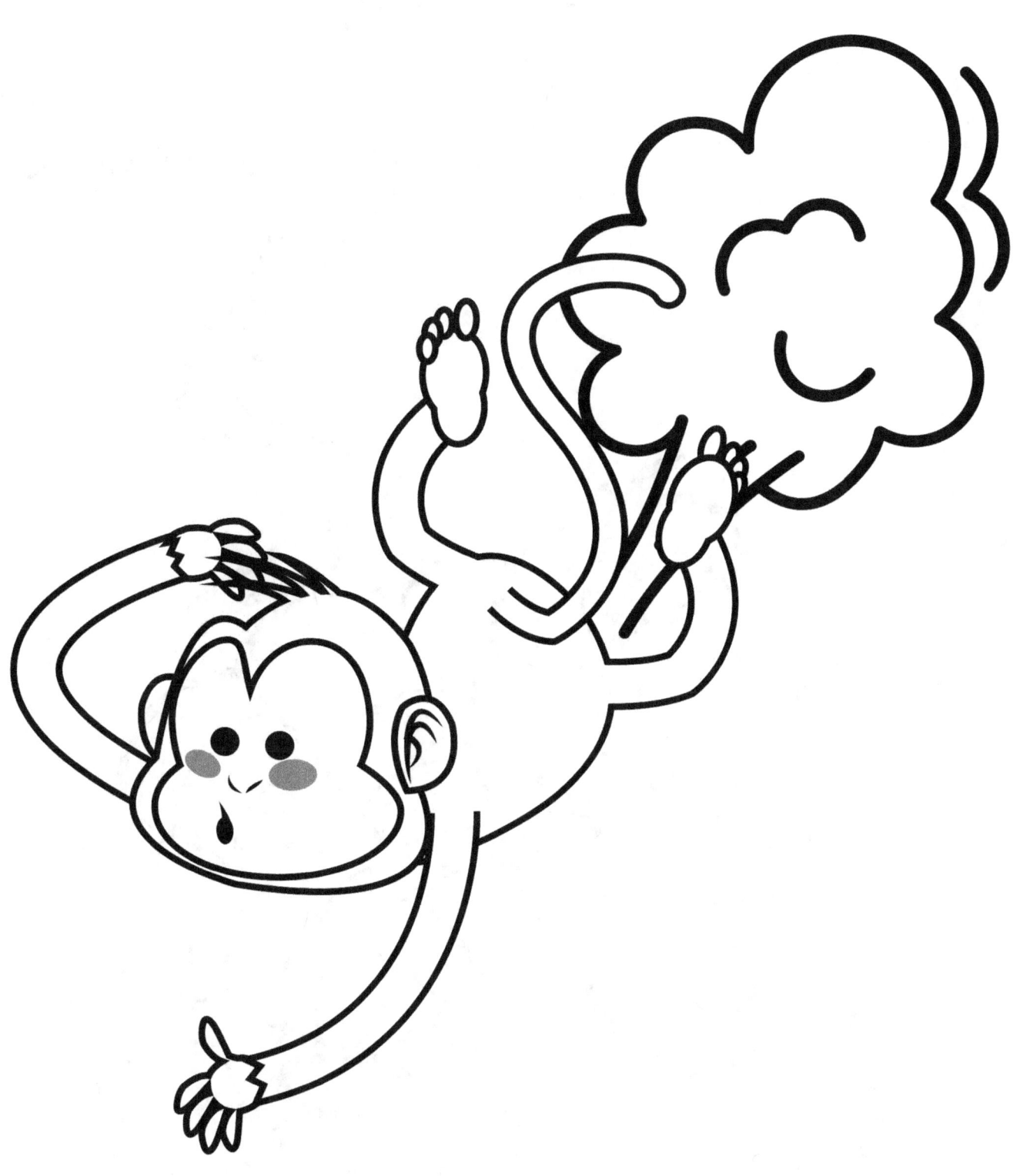

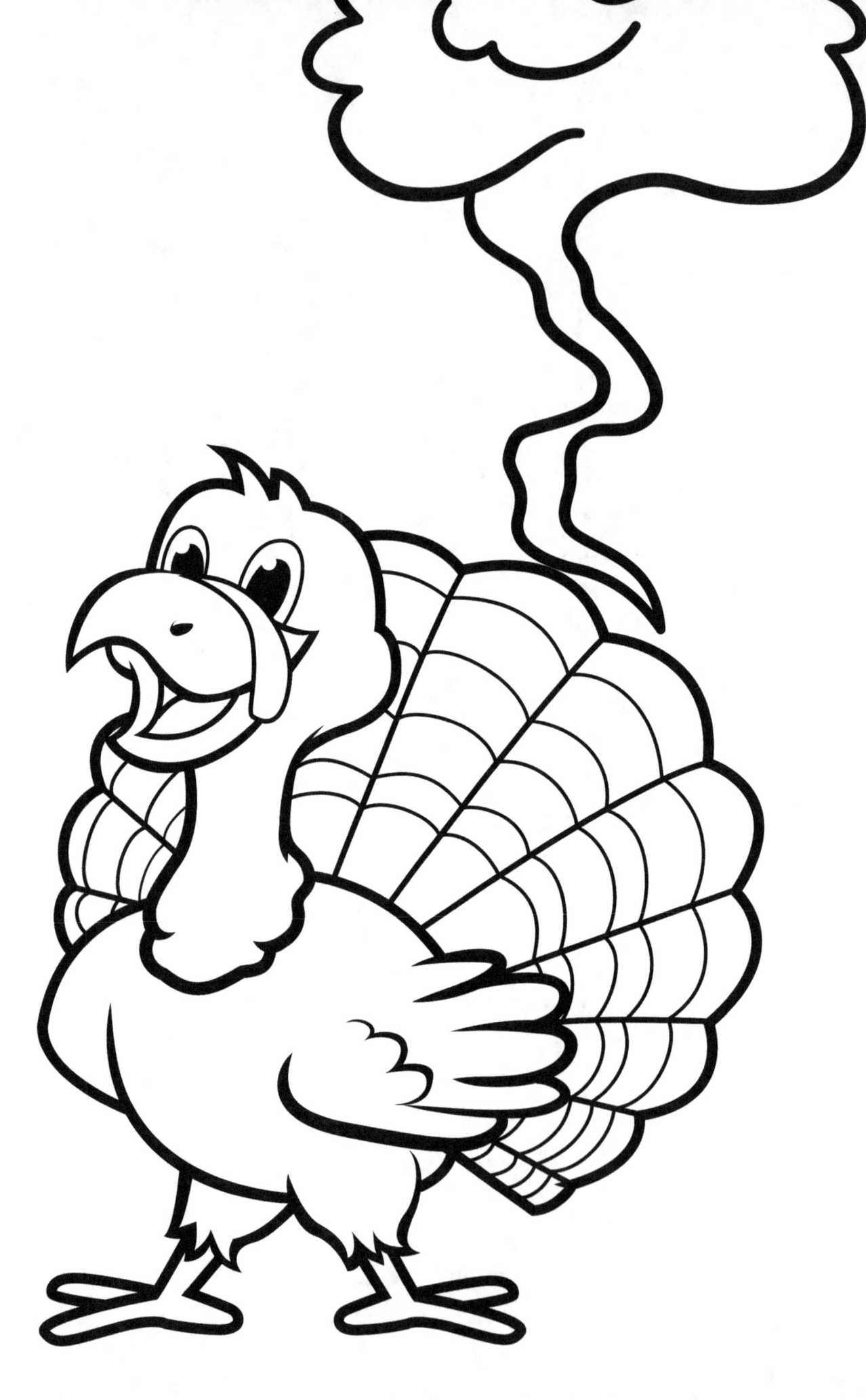

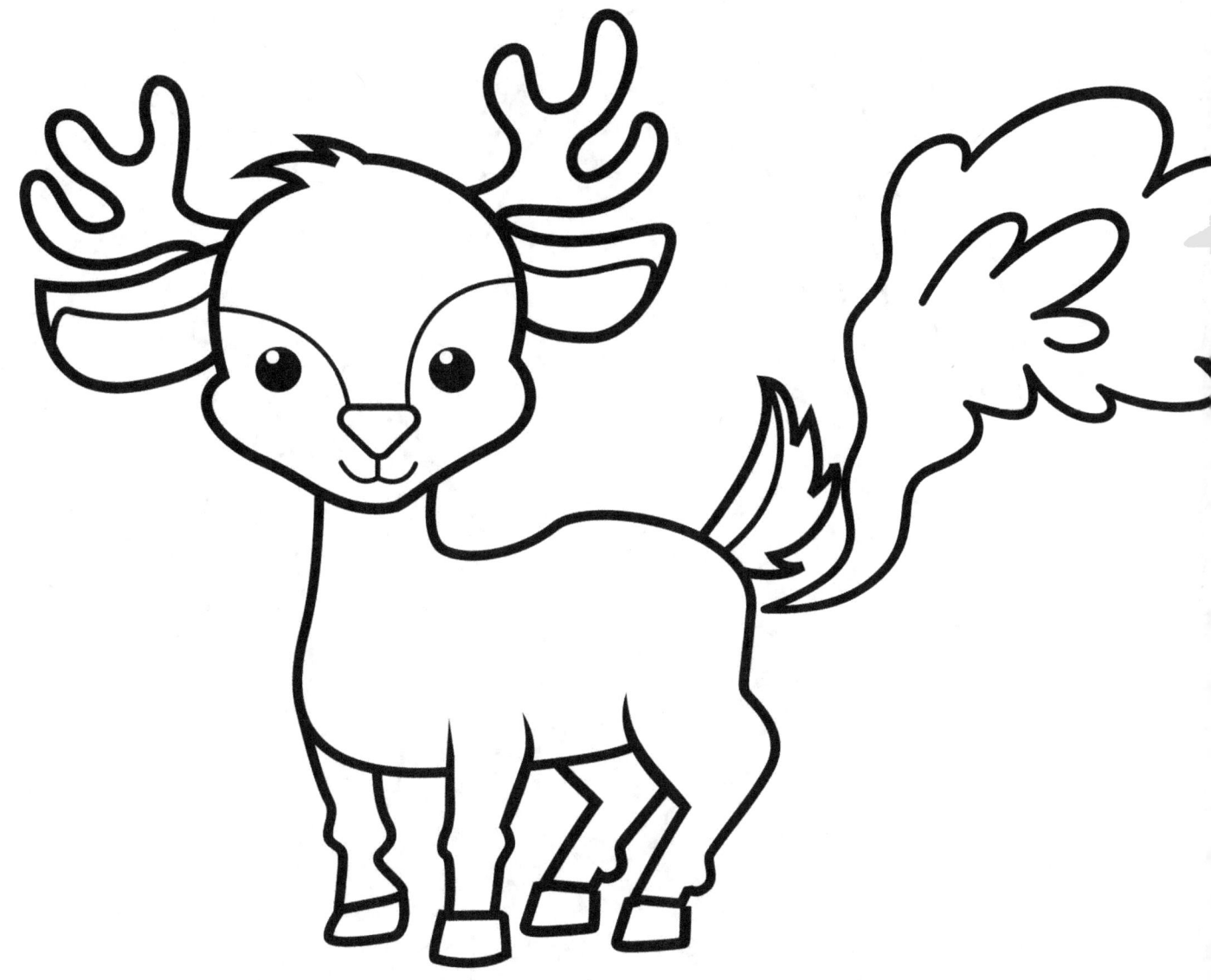

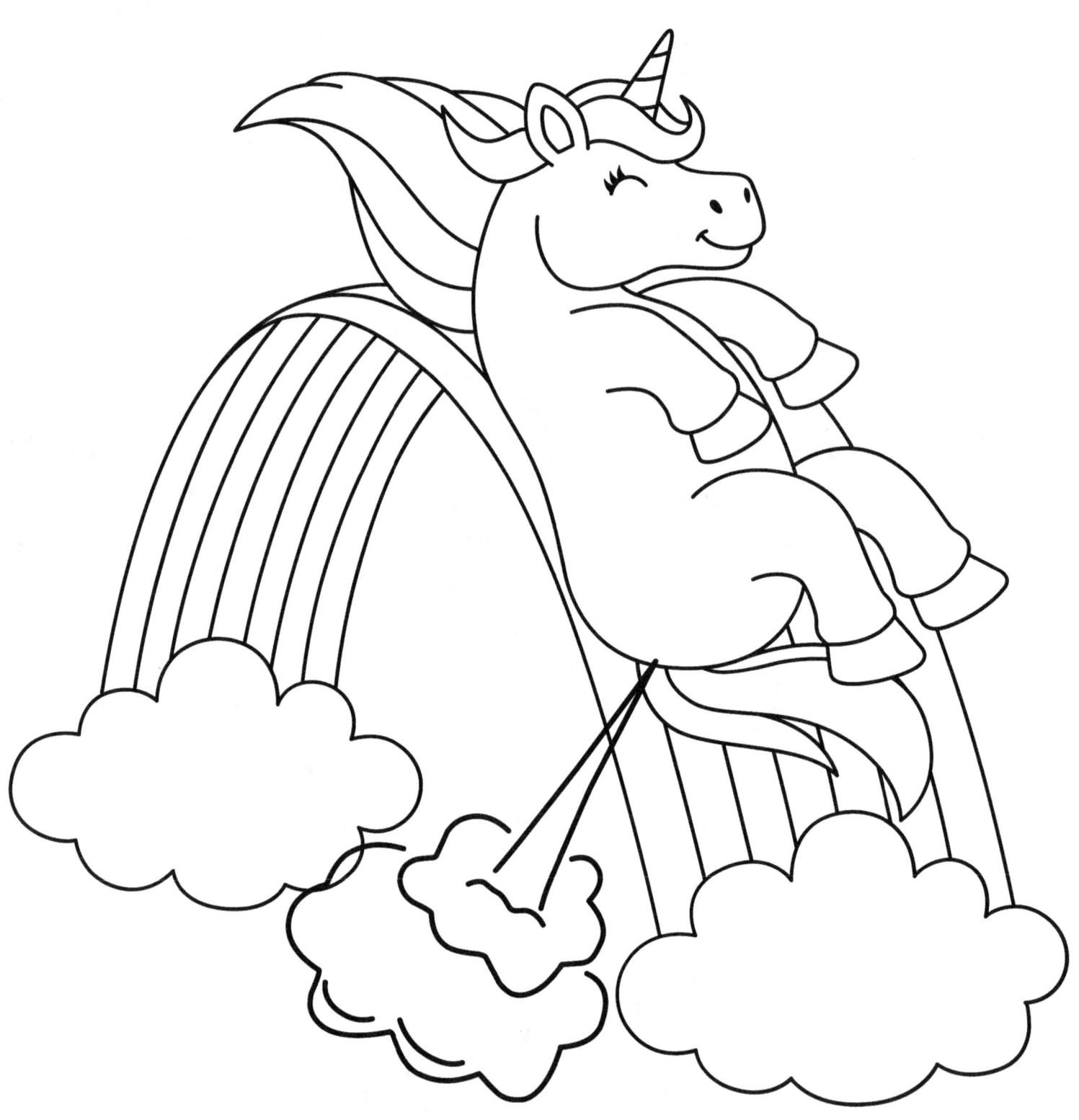

# MAYBE GLITTER ISN'T THE ONLY THING THIS UNICORN CAN MAKE APPEAR!

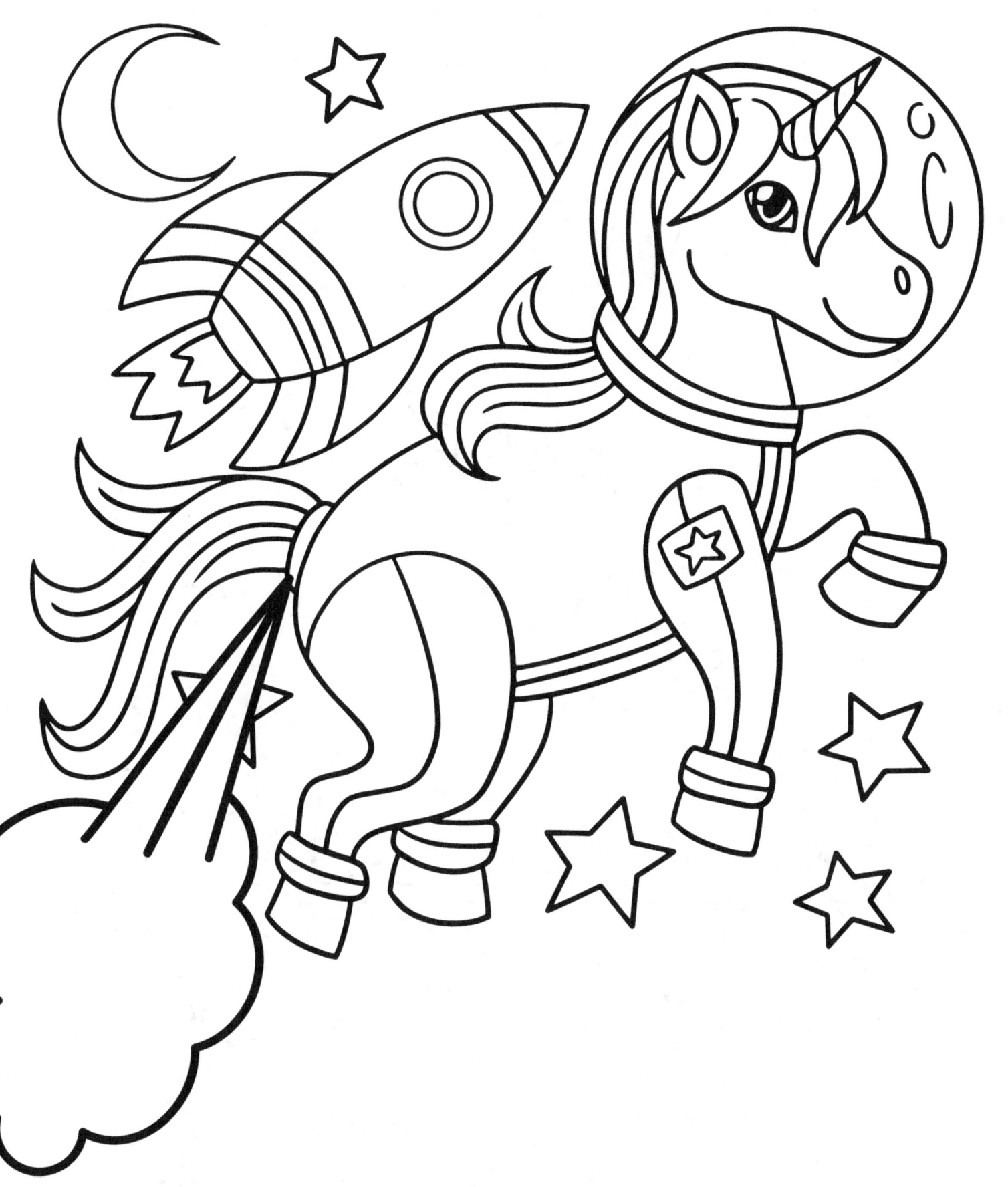

# OUT OF THIS WORLD

# DREAM LIKE A UNICORN

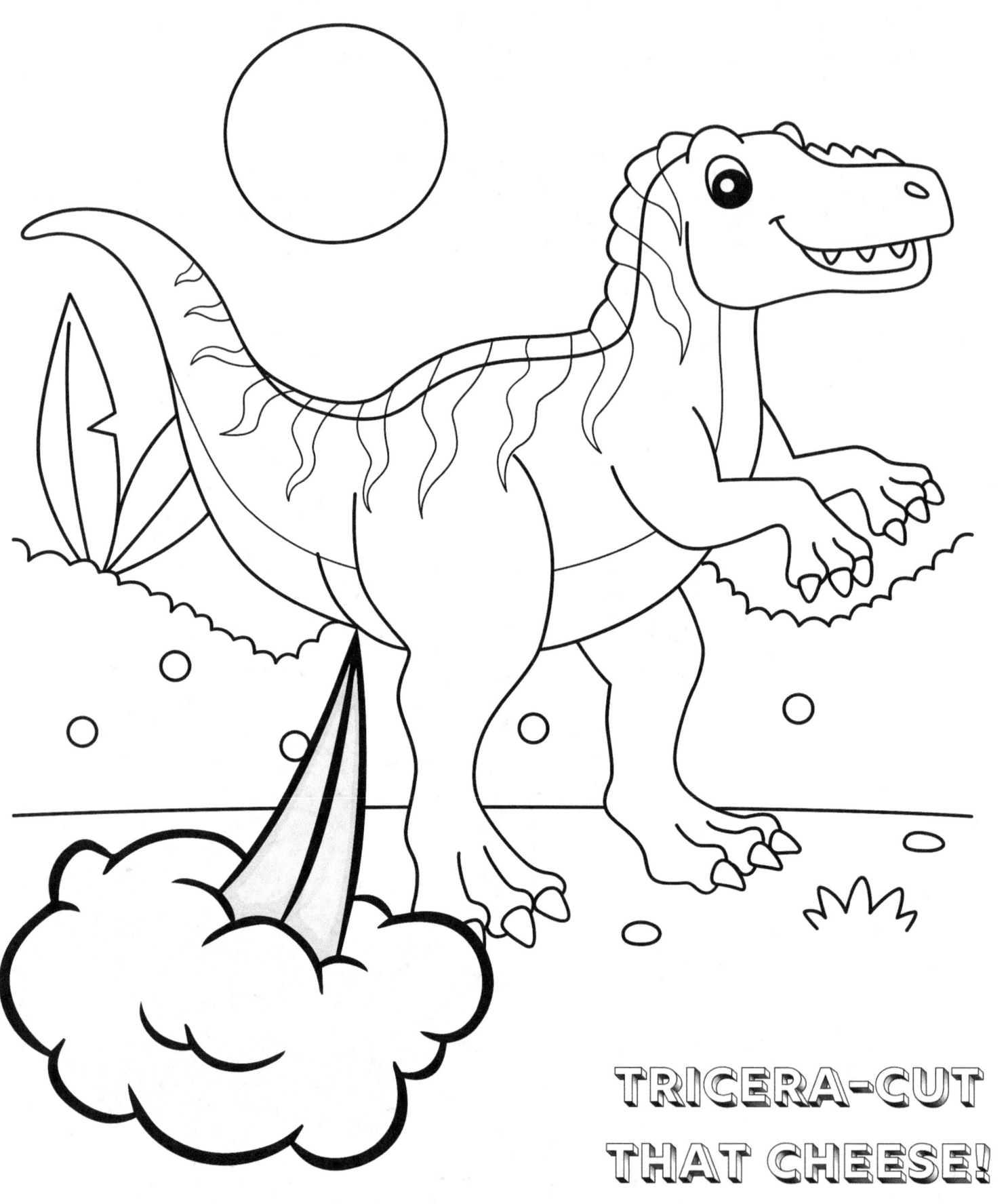

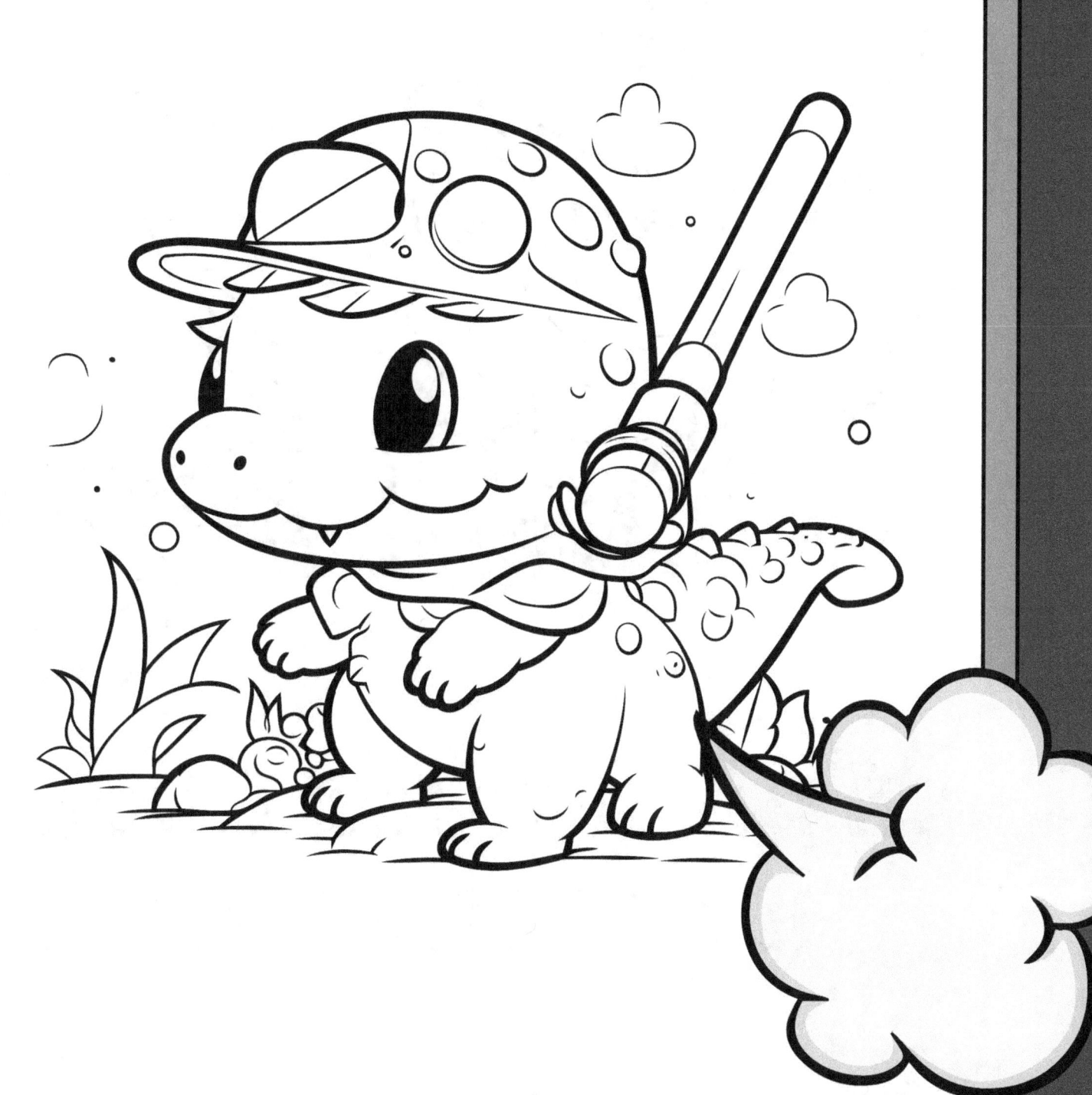

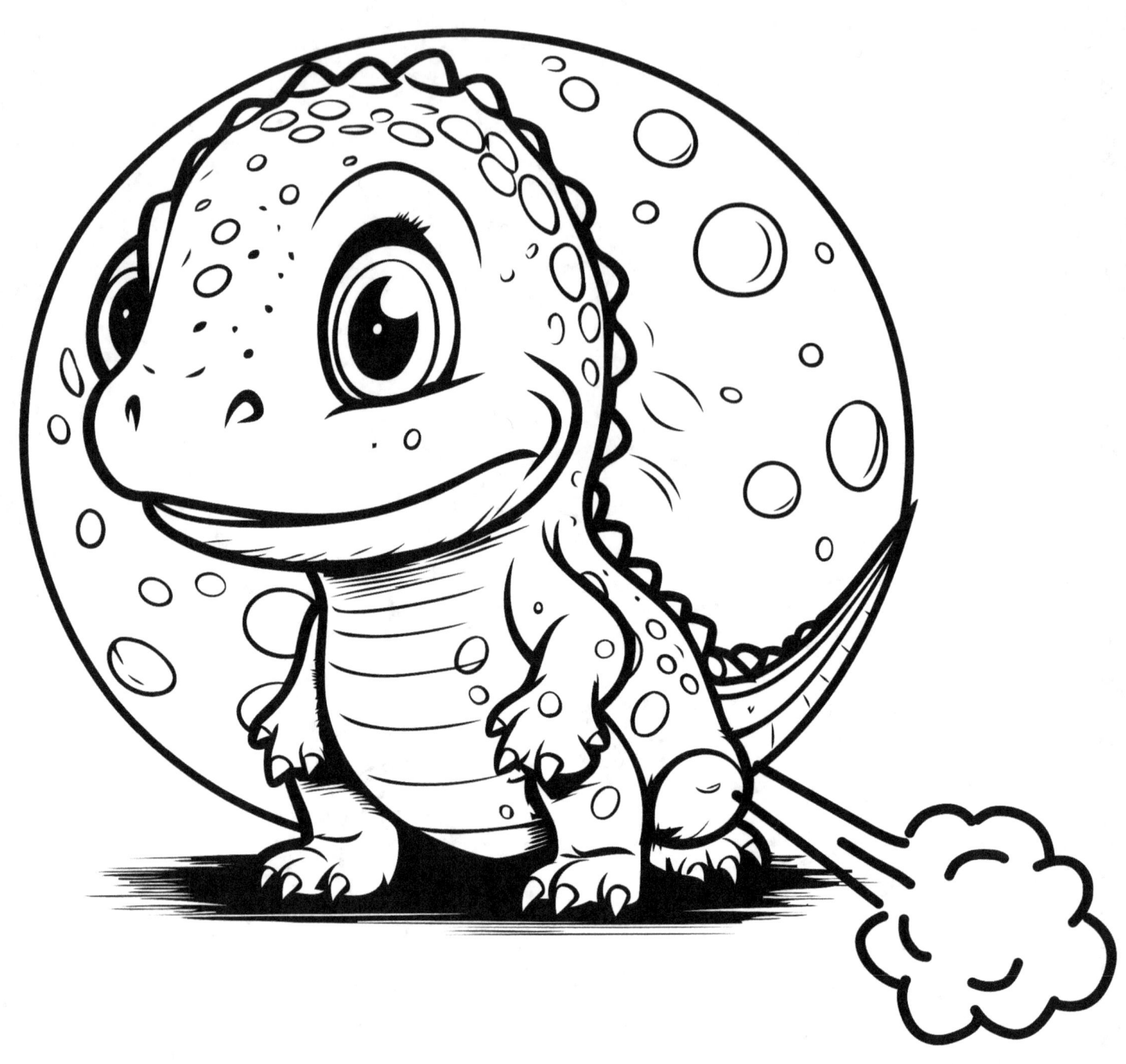

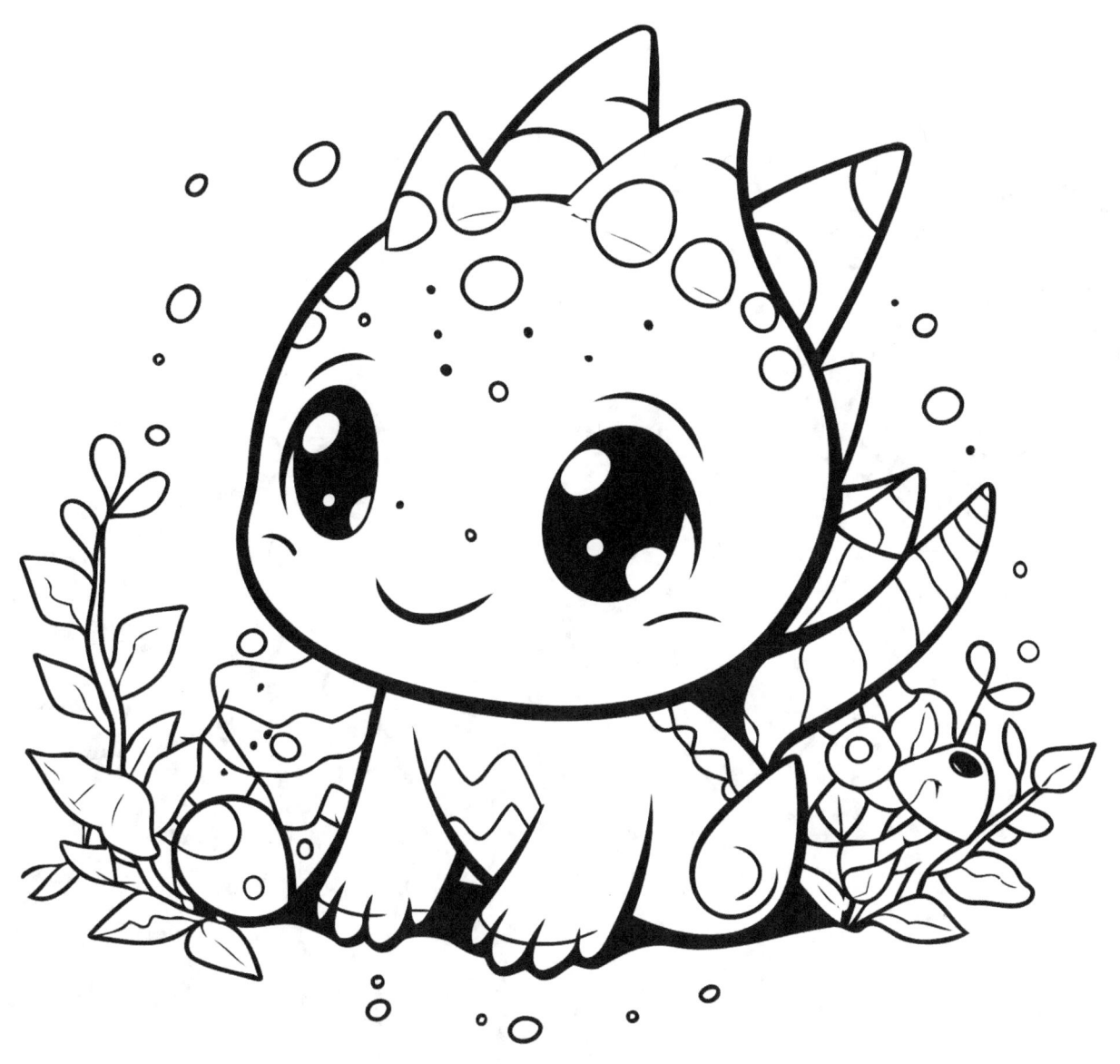

"JUST A LITTLE PTERAN-TOOT TO GET THE DAY STARTED!"

"BRACHIOSAURUS LETTING LOOSE A LONG, LOW RUMBLE."

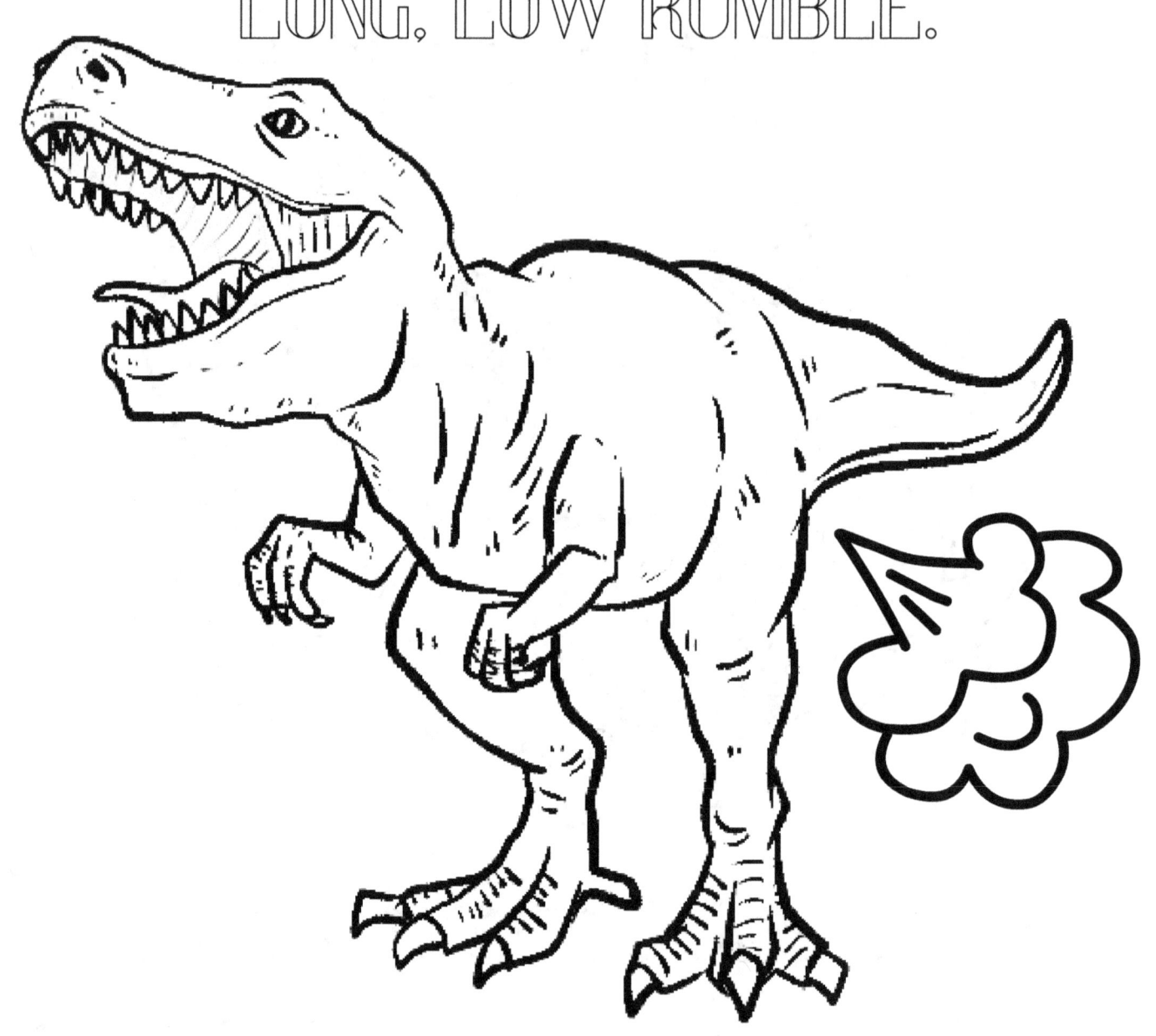

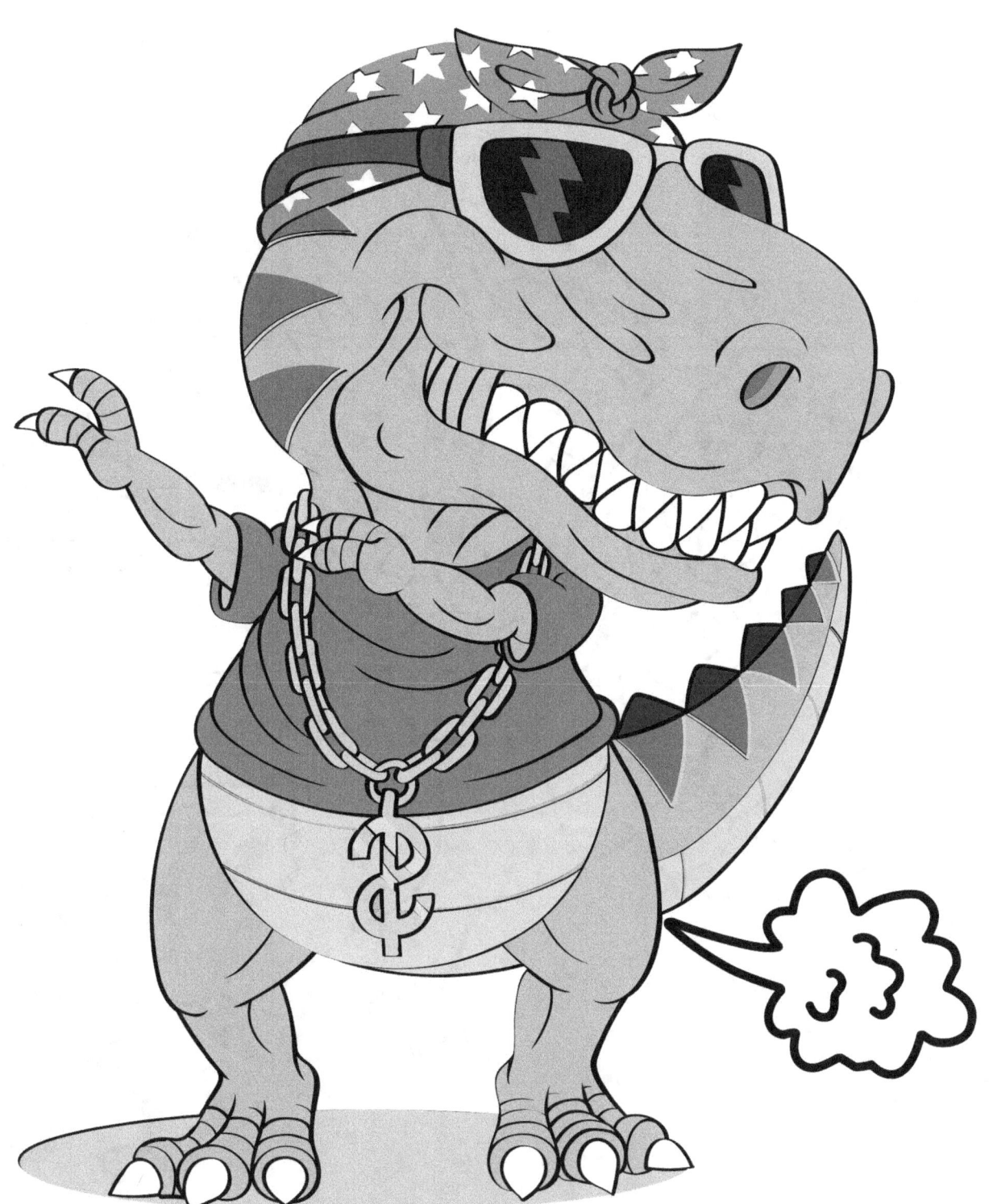

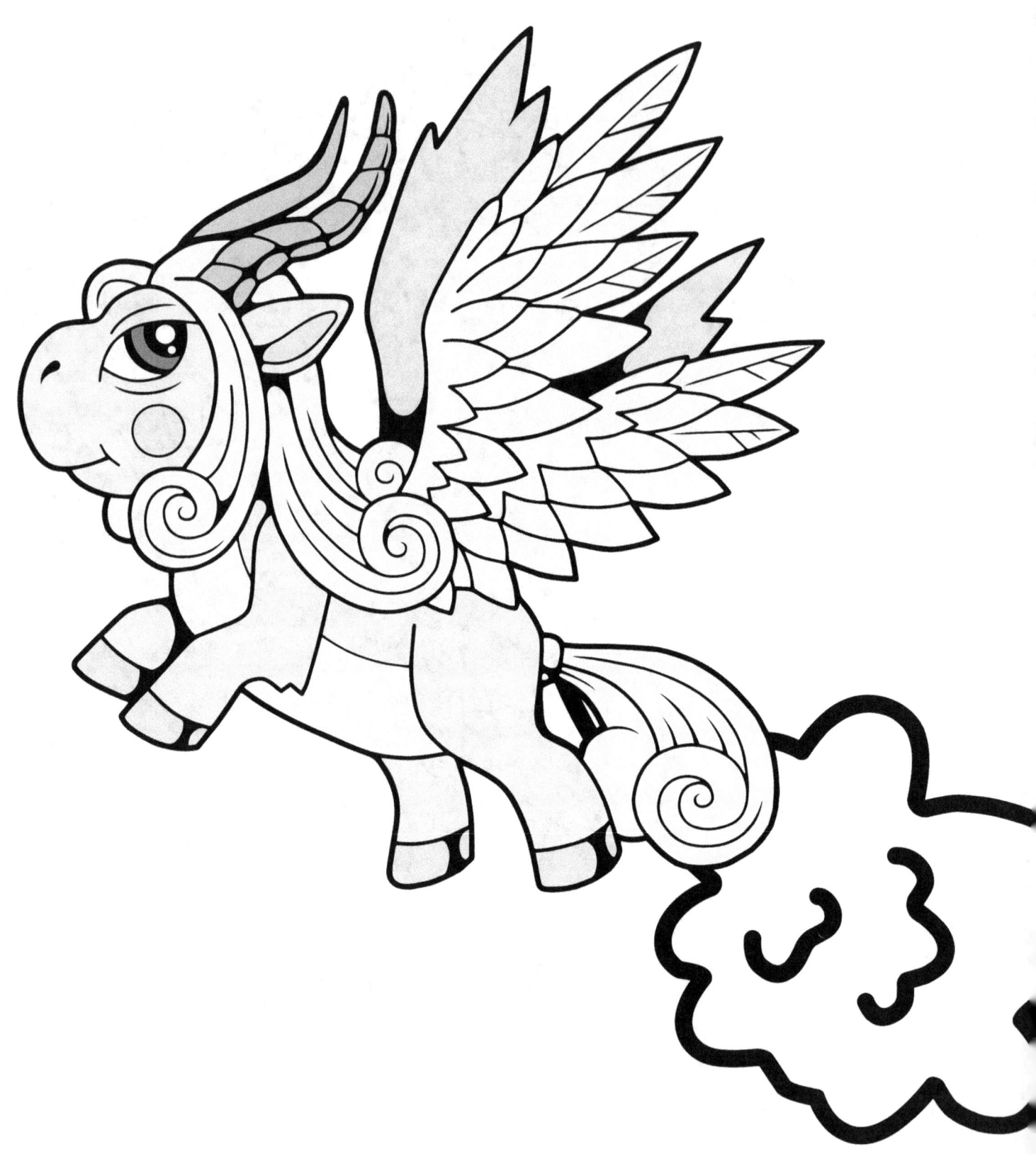

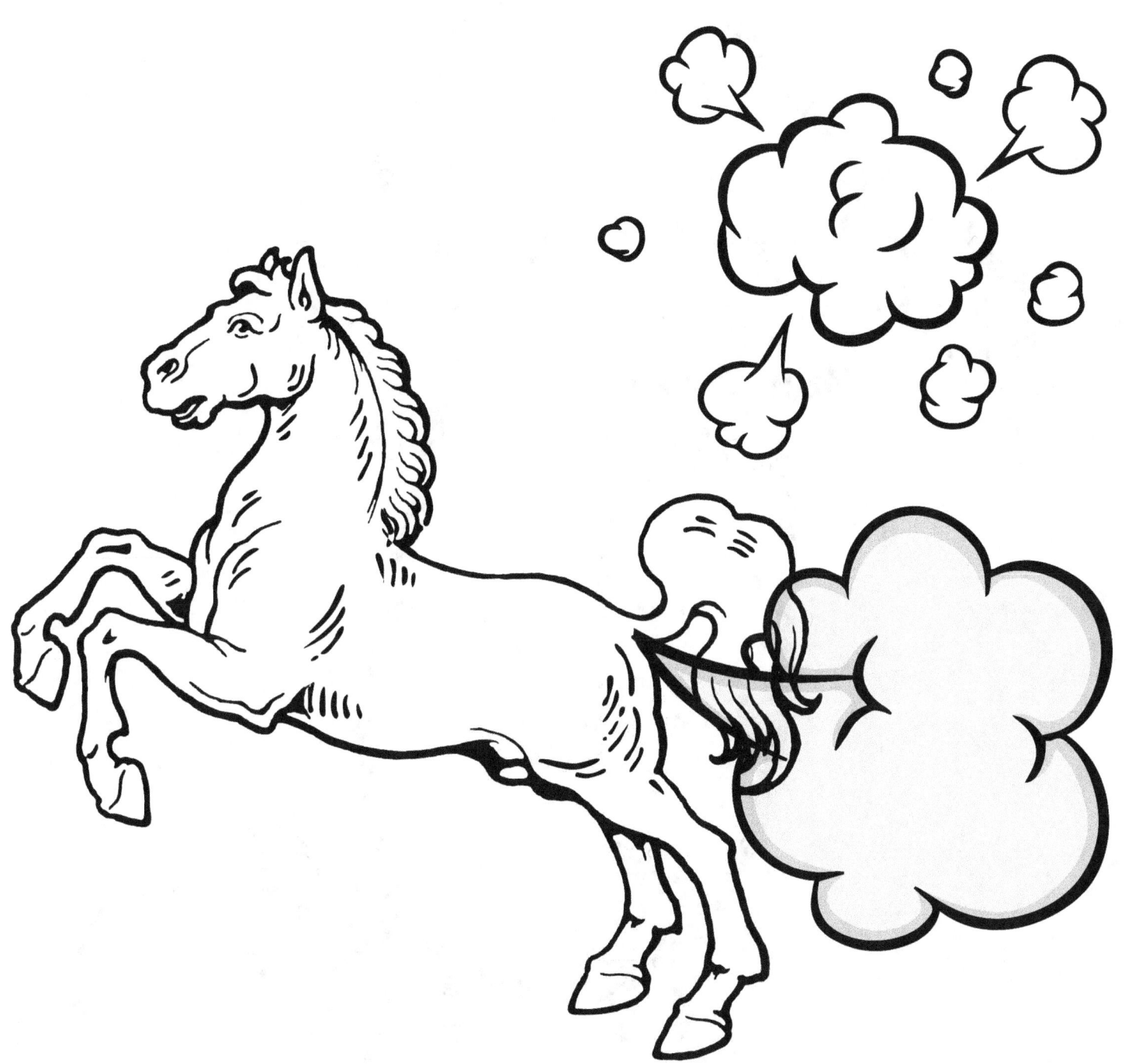

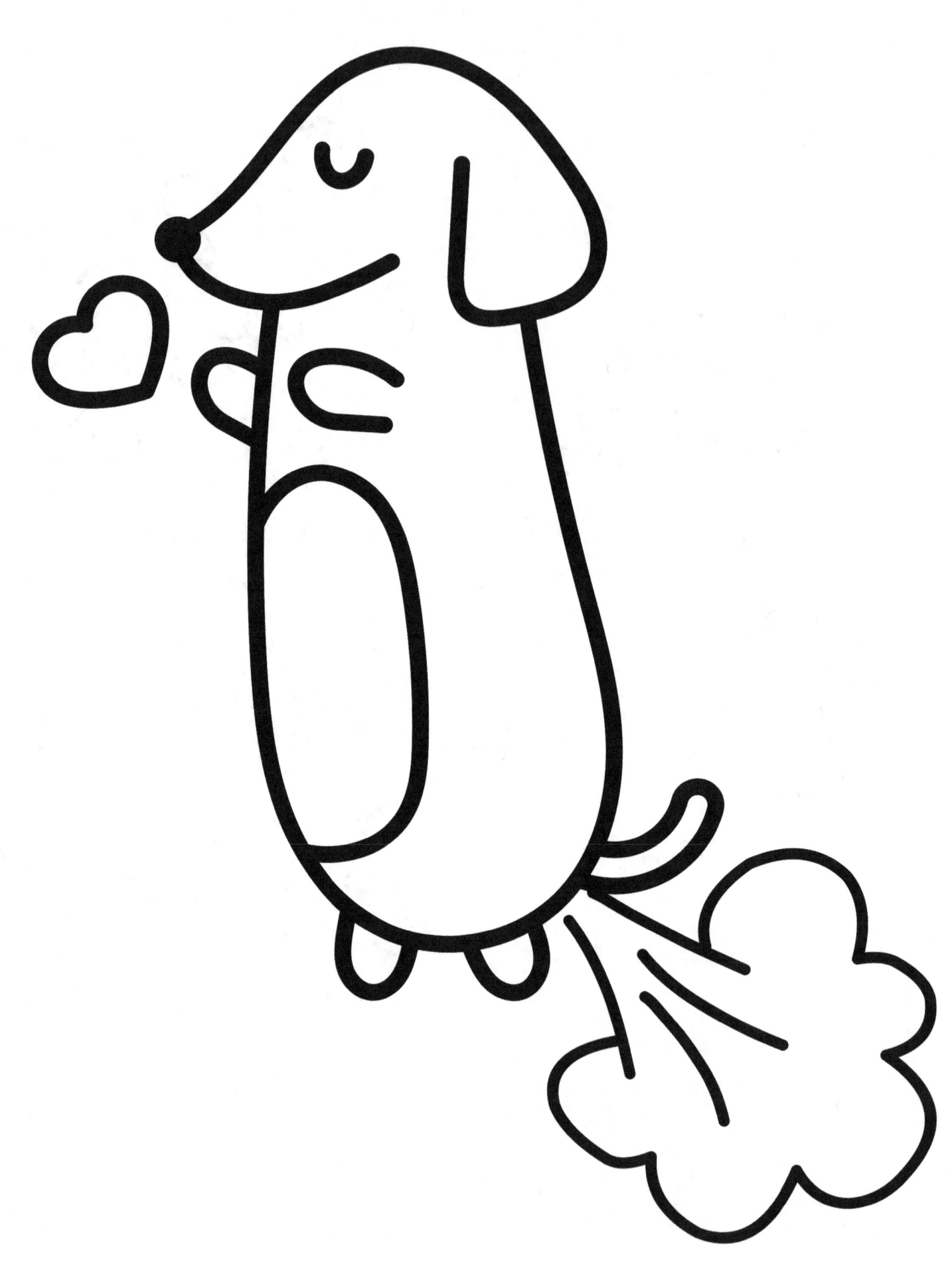

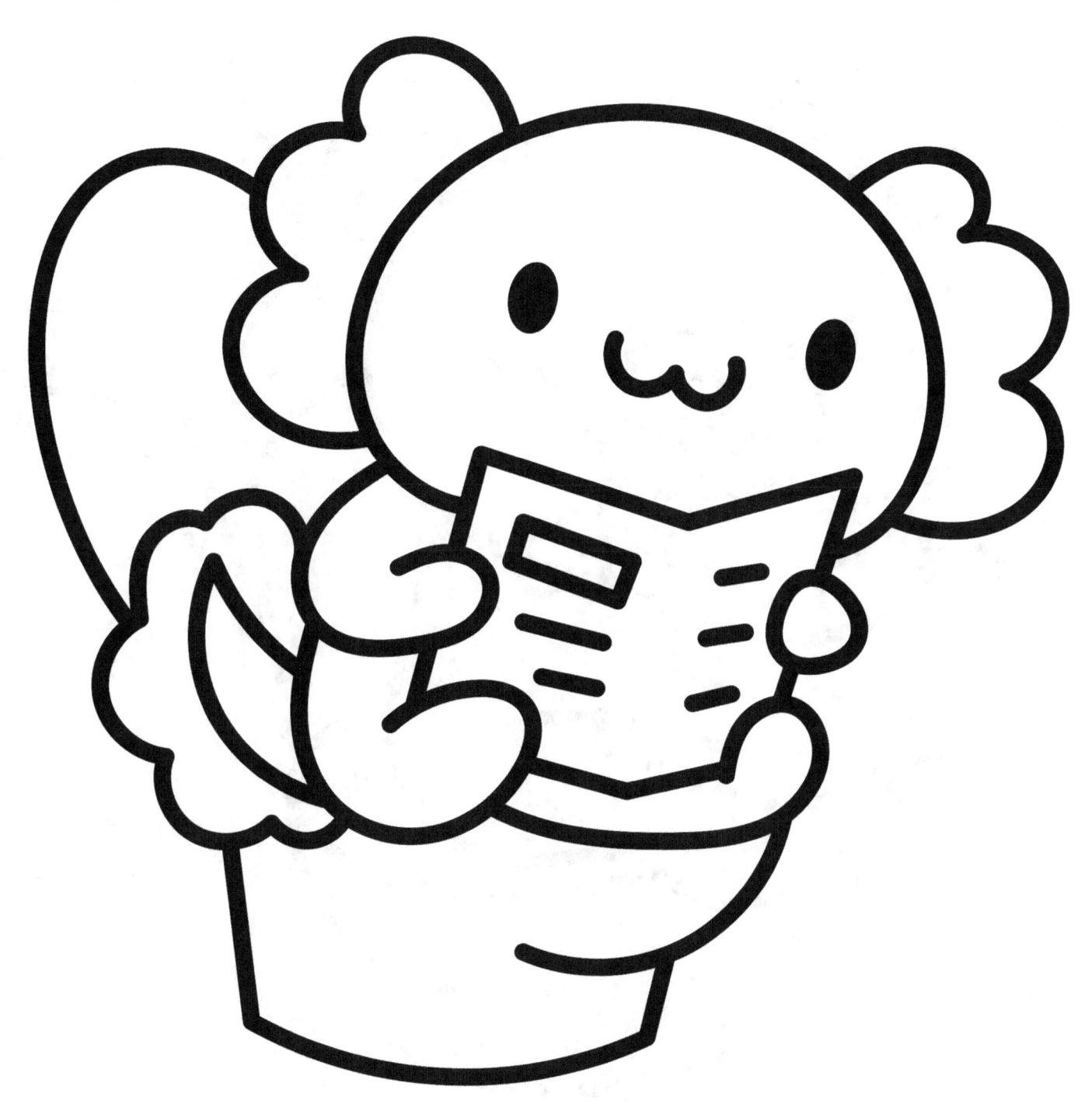

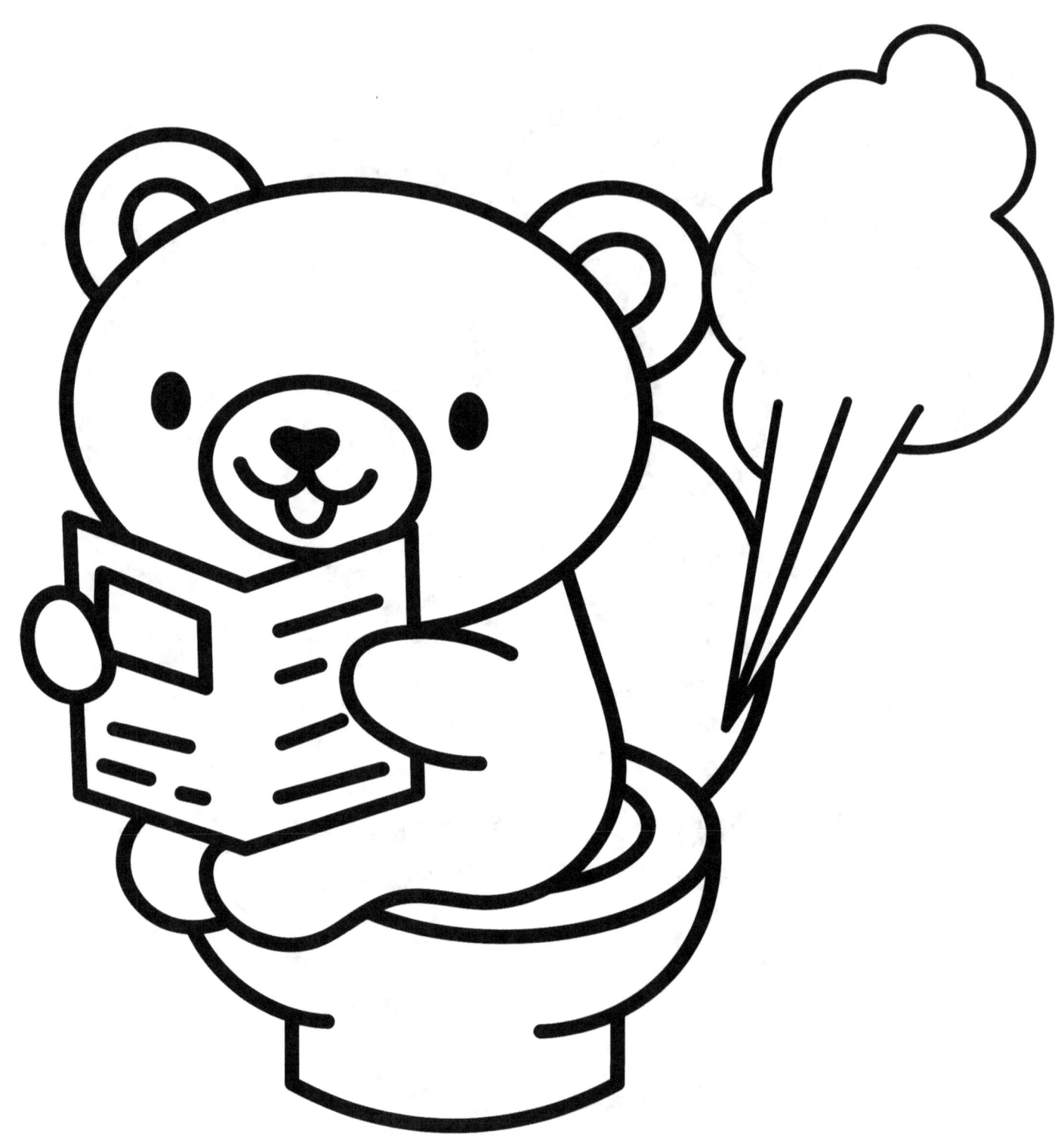

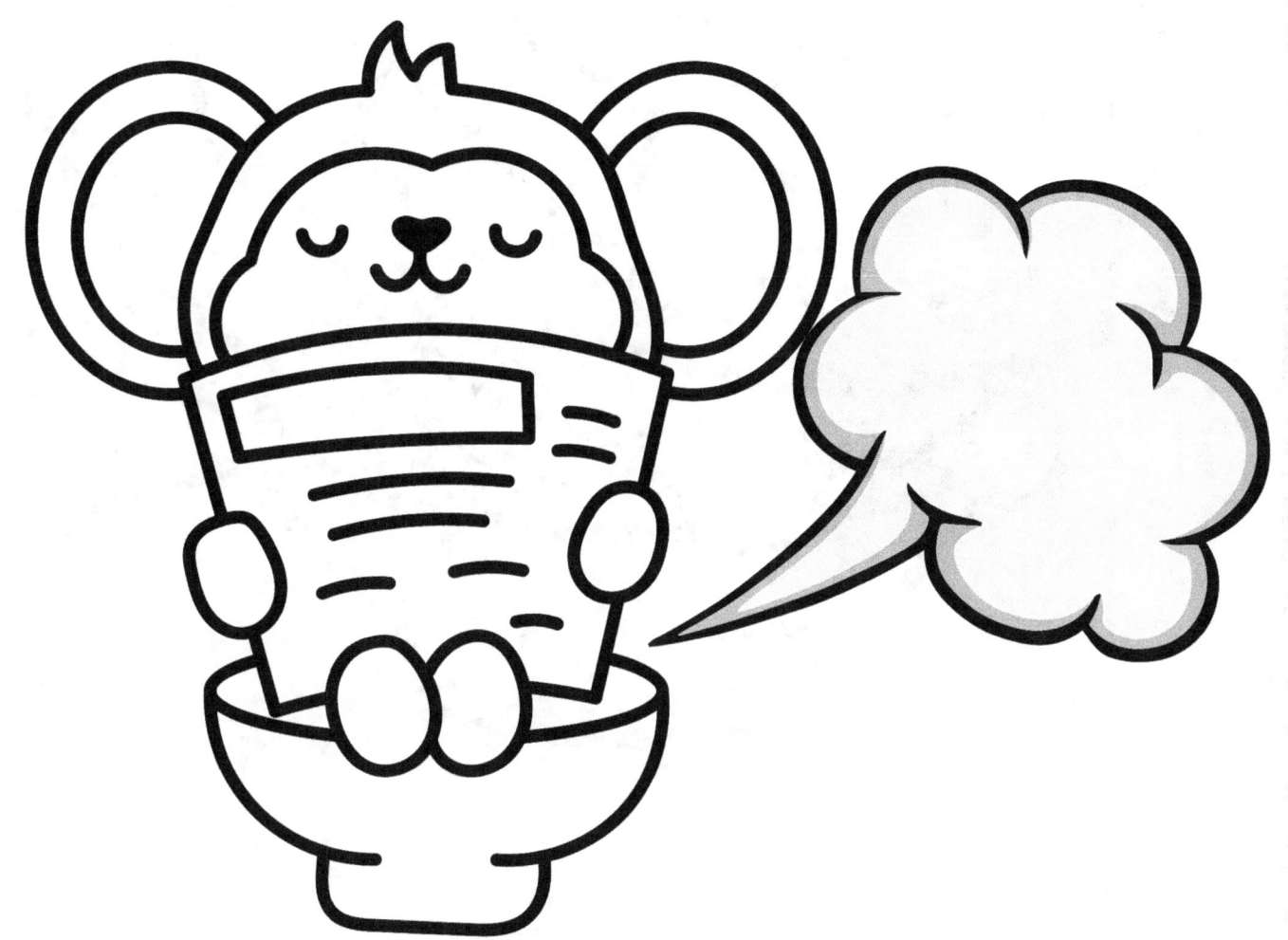

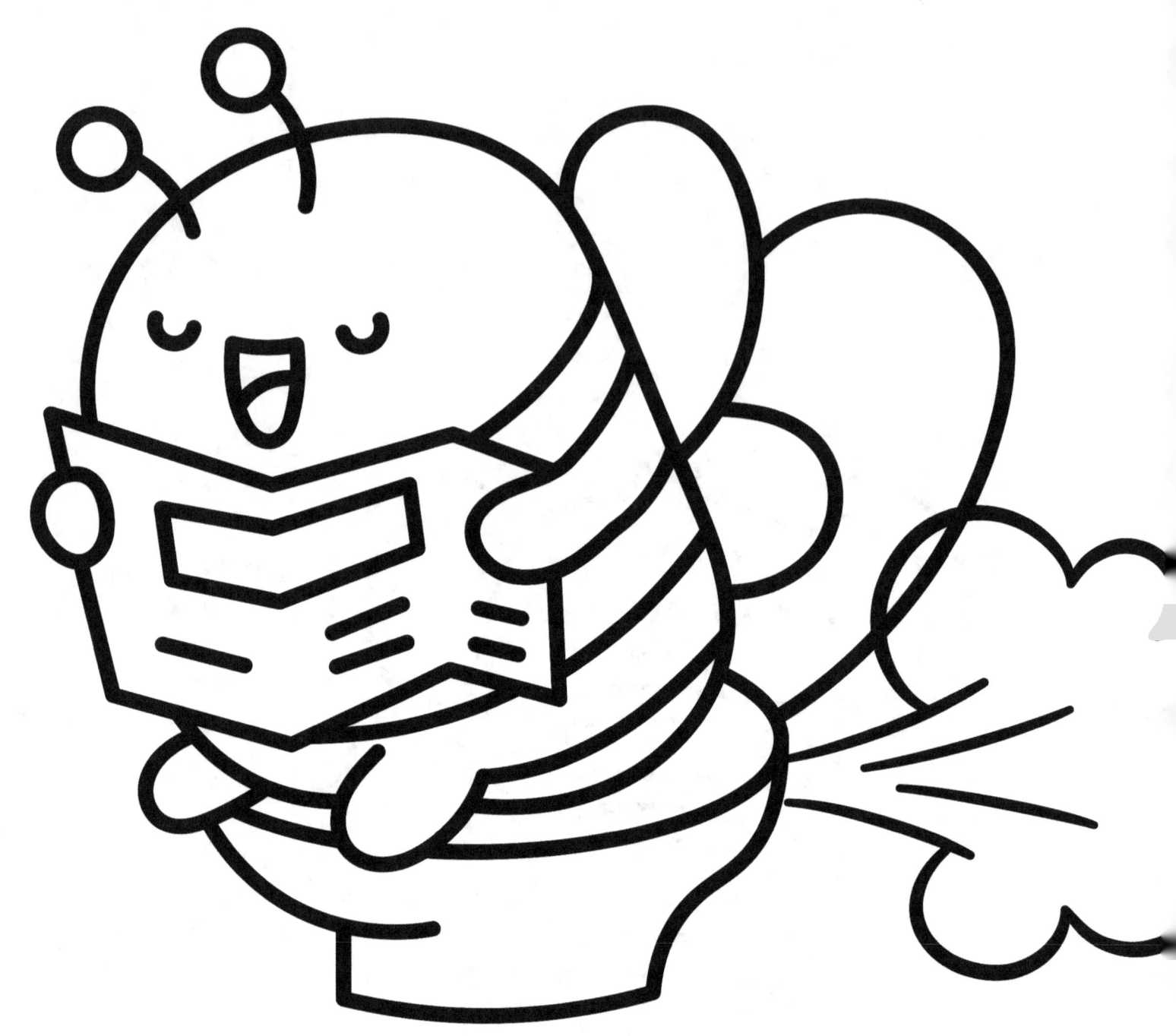

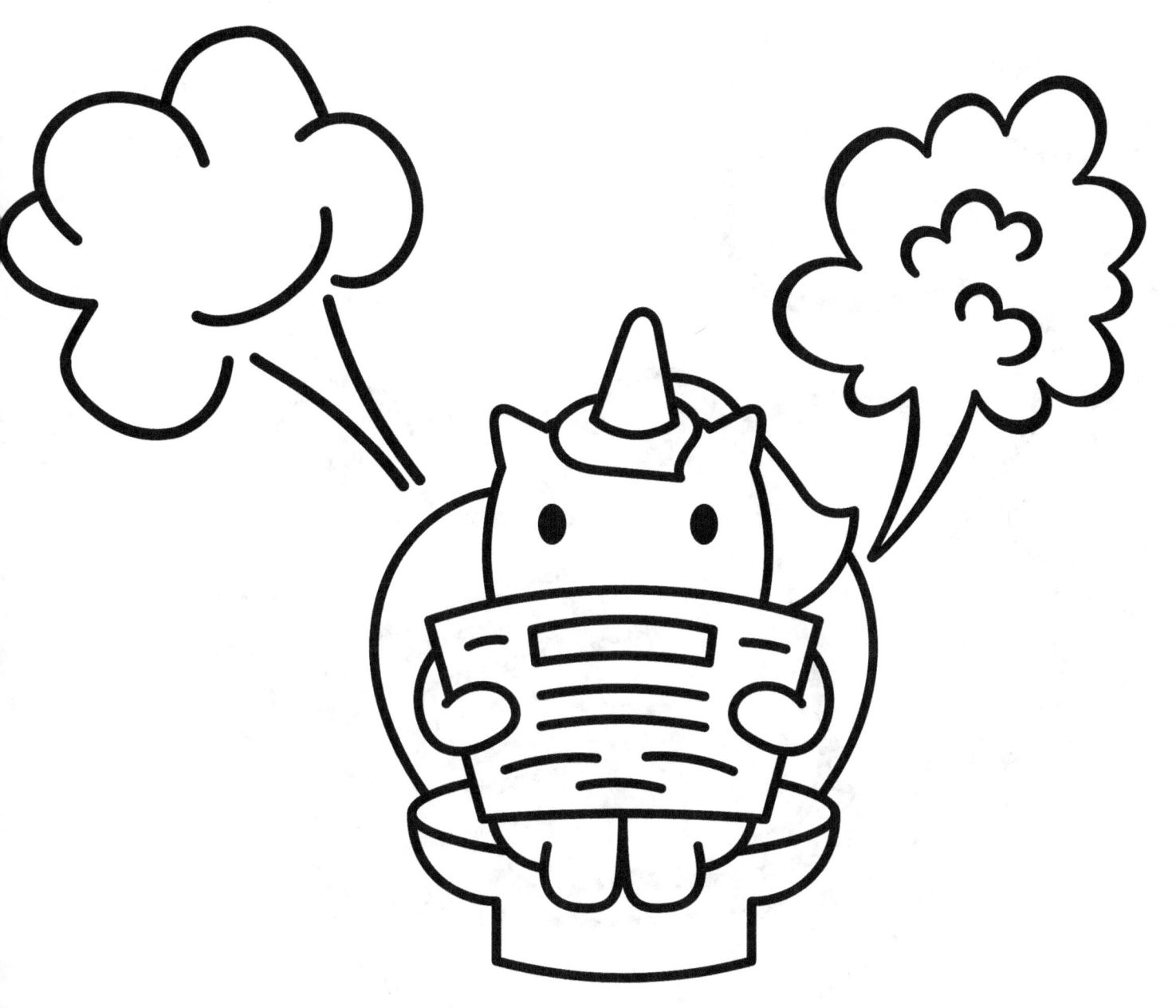

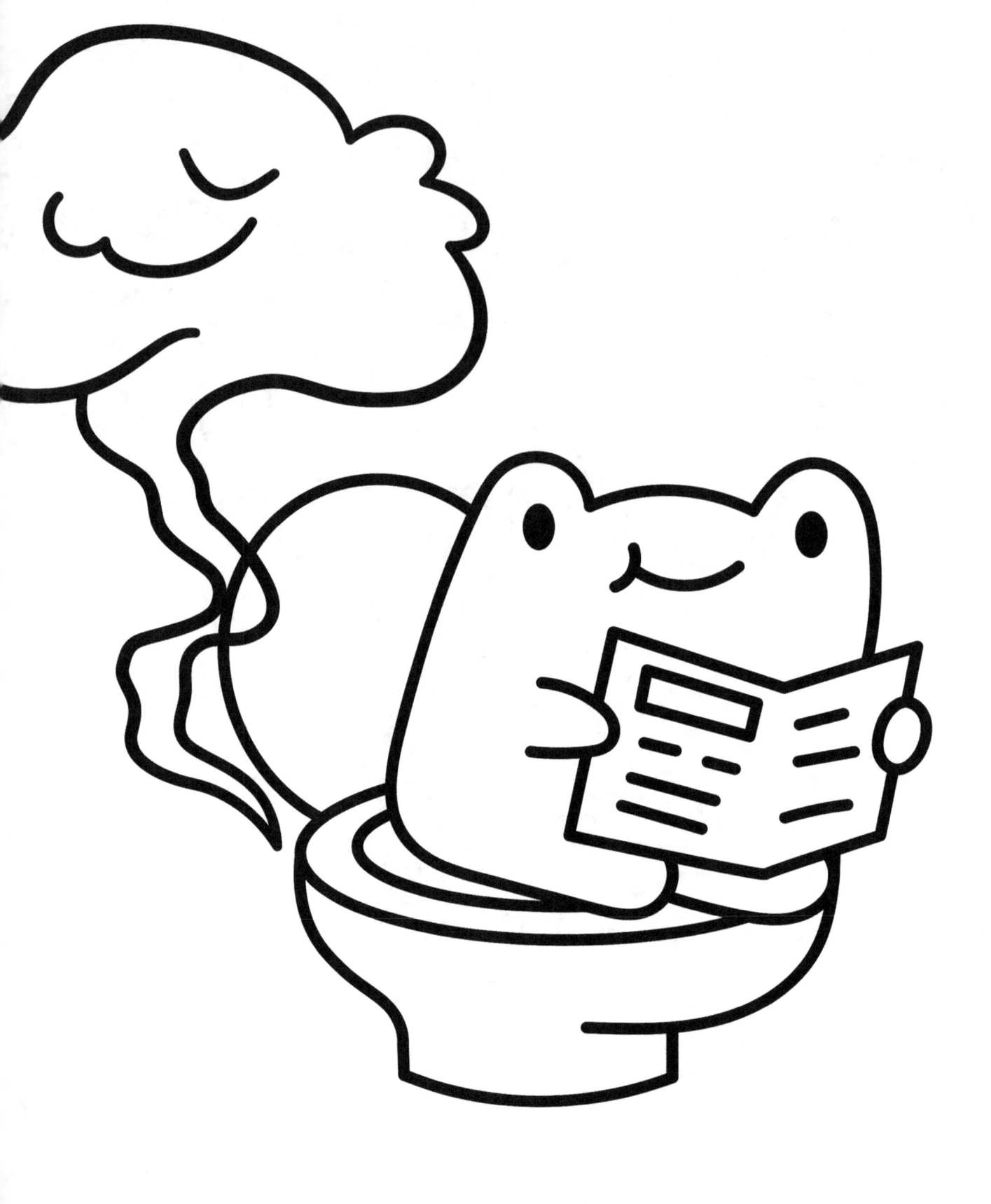

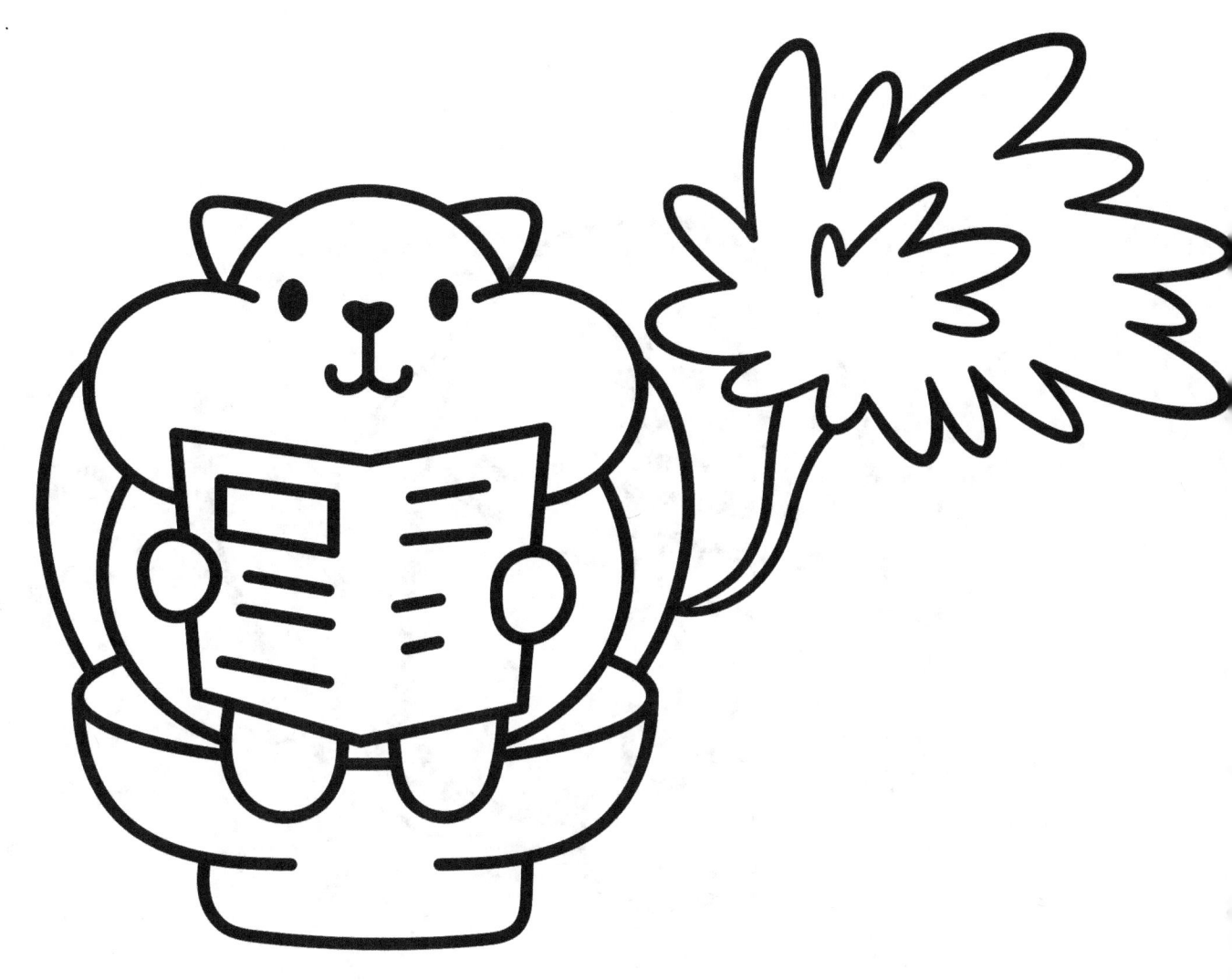

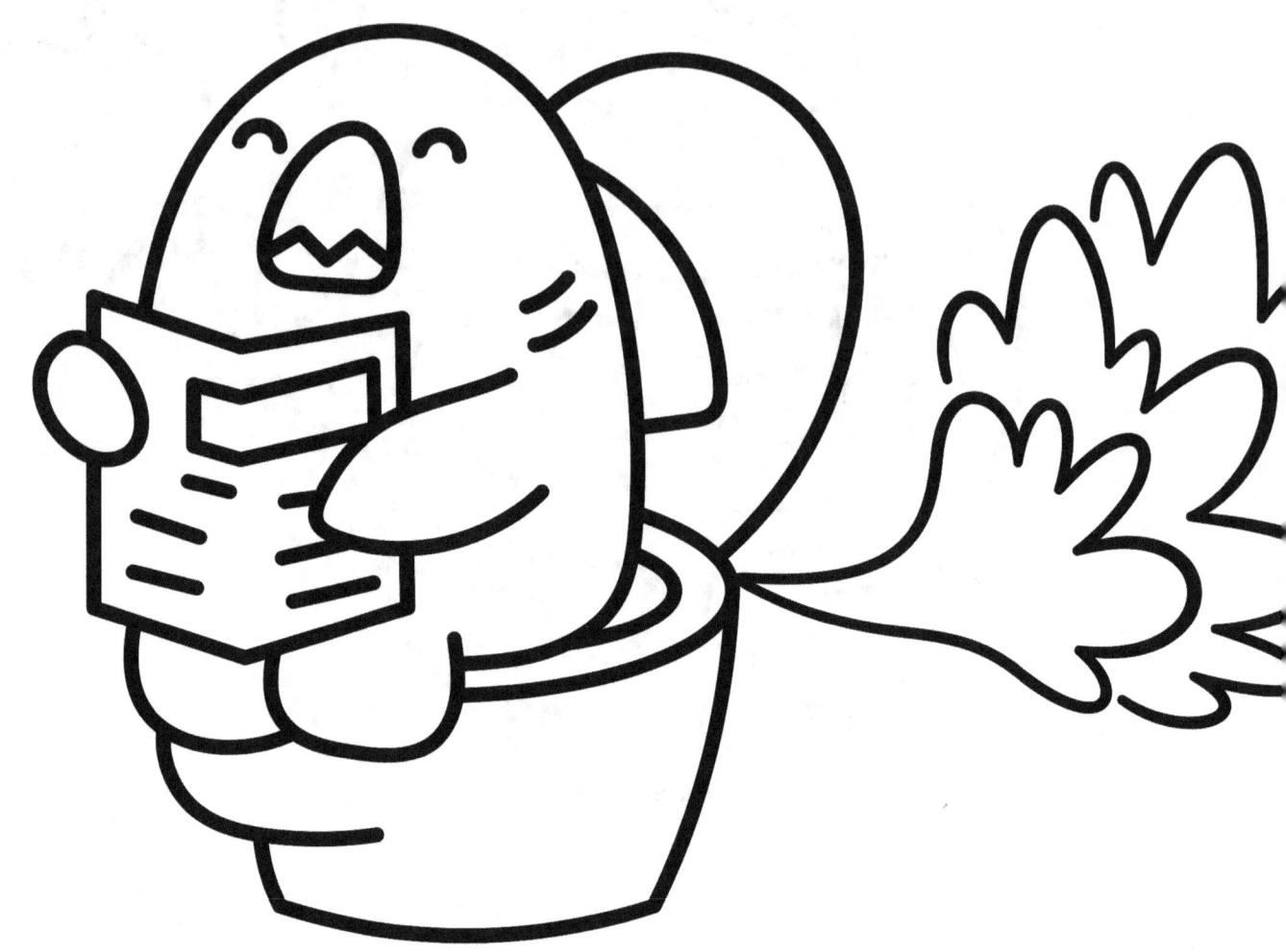

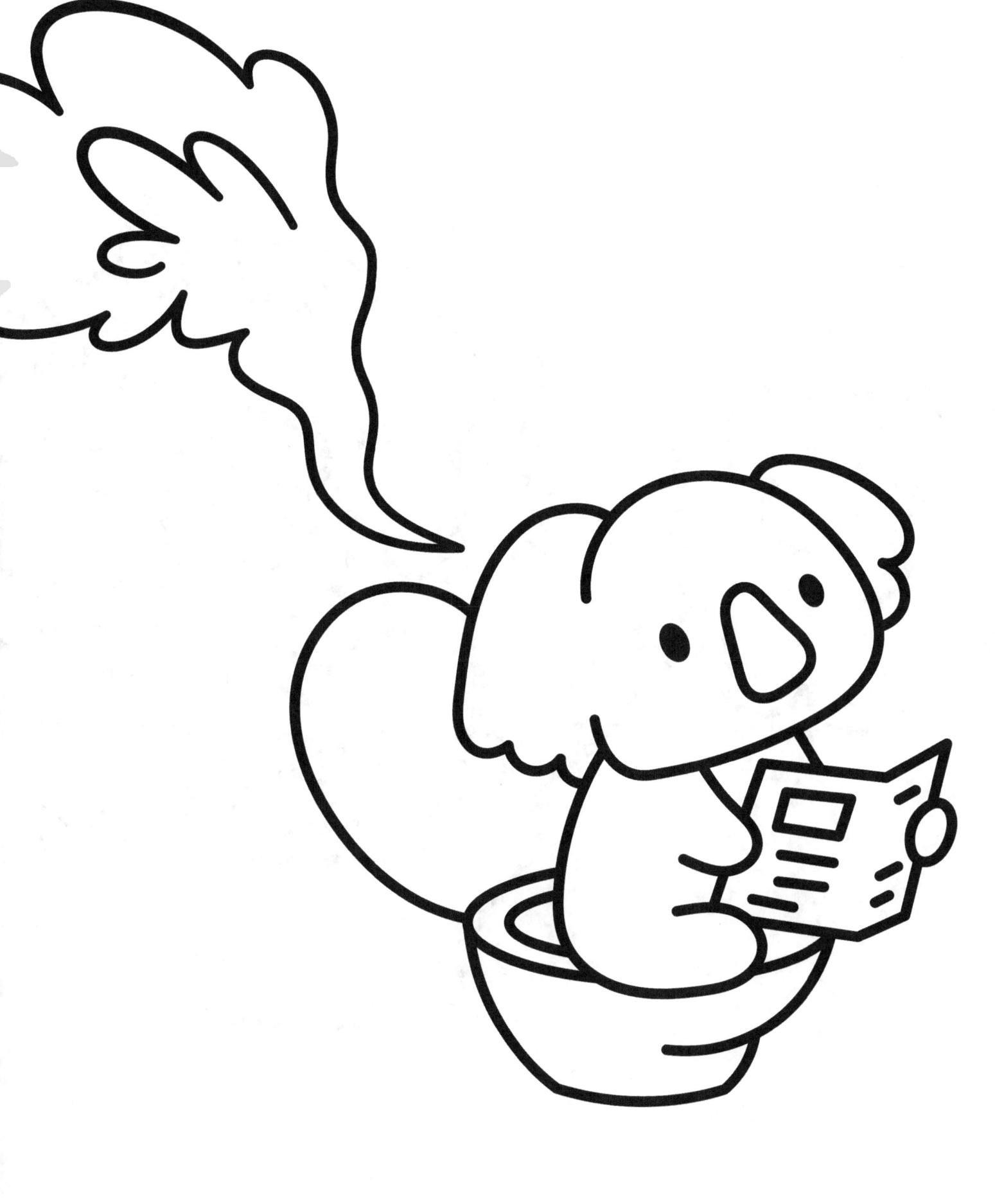

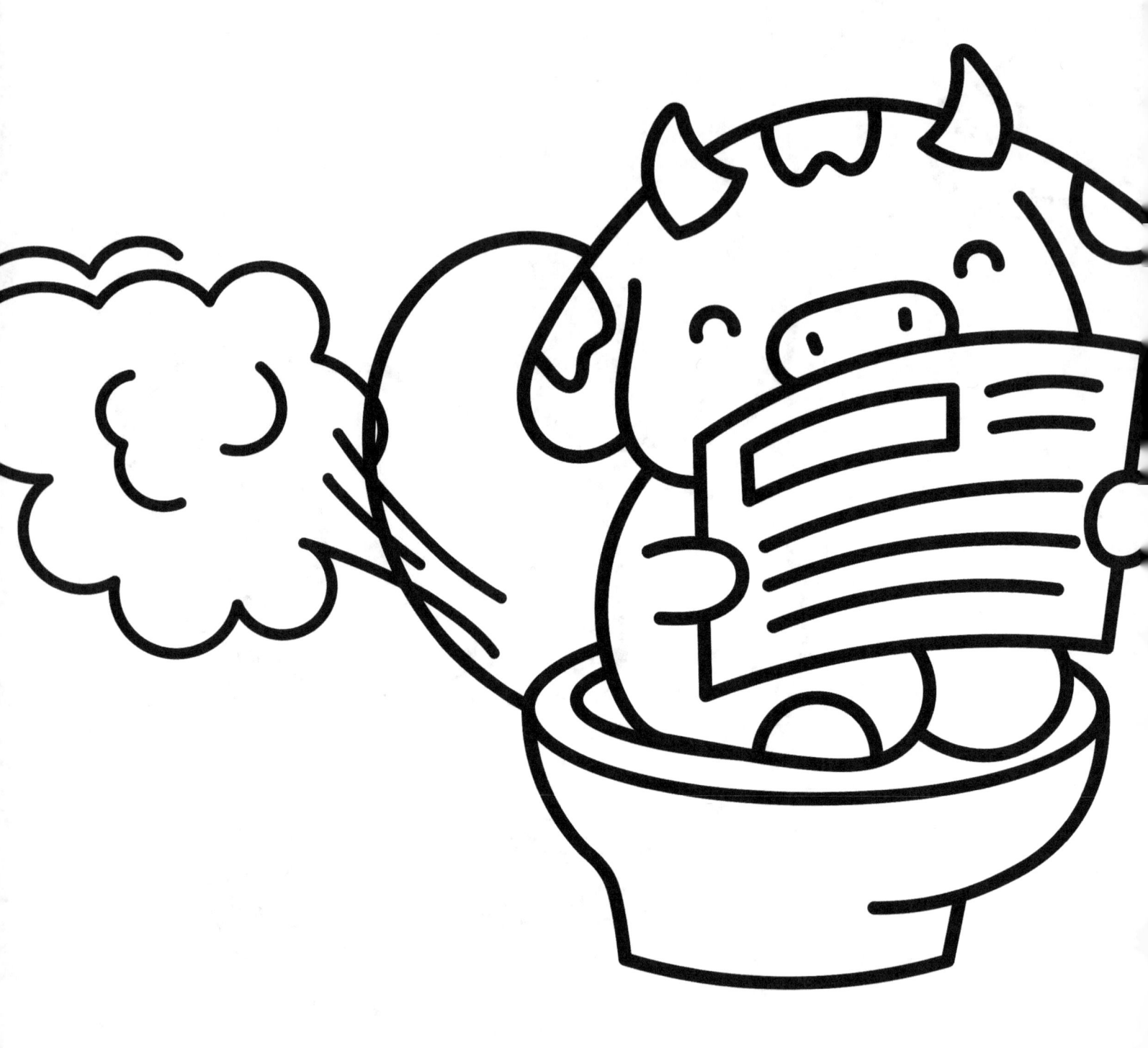

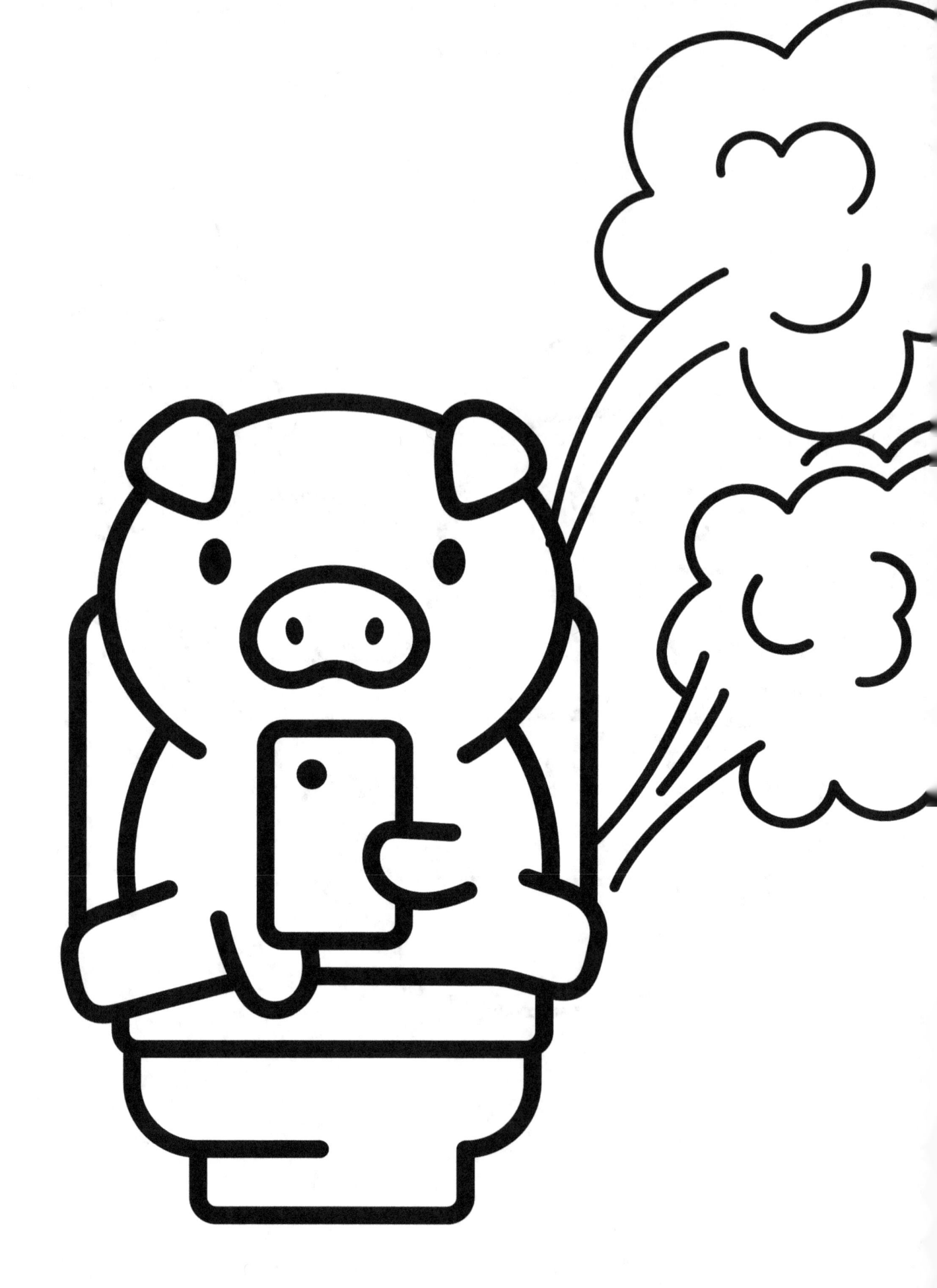

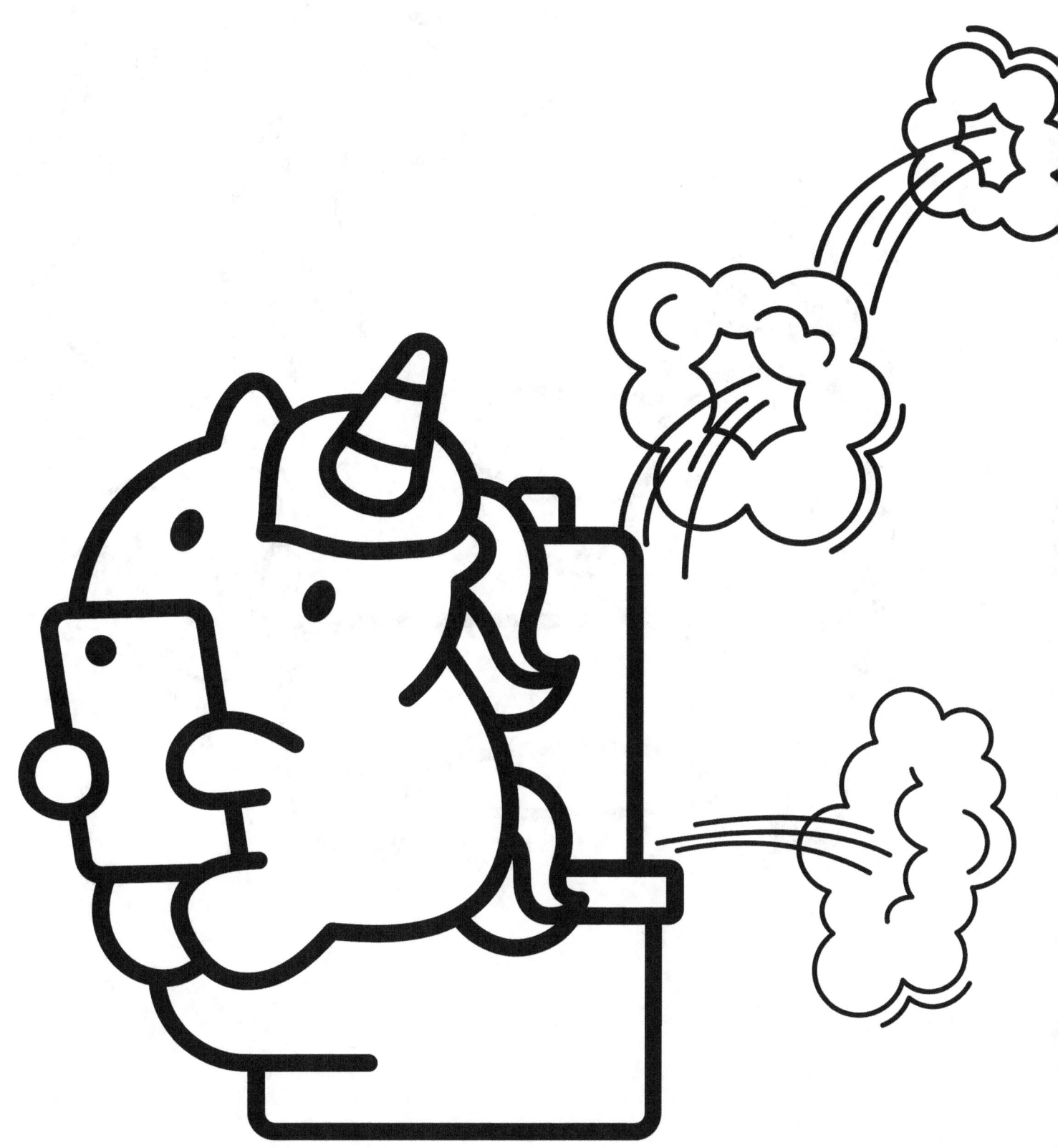

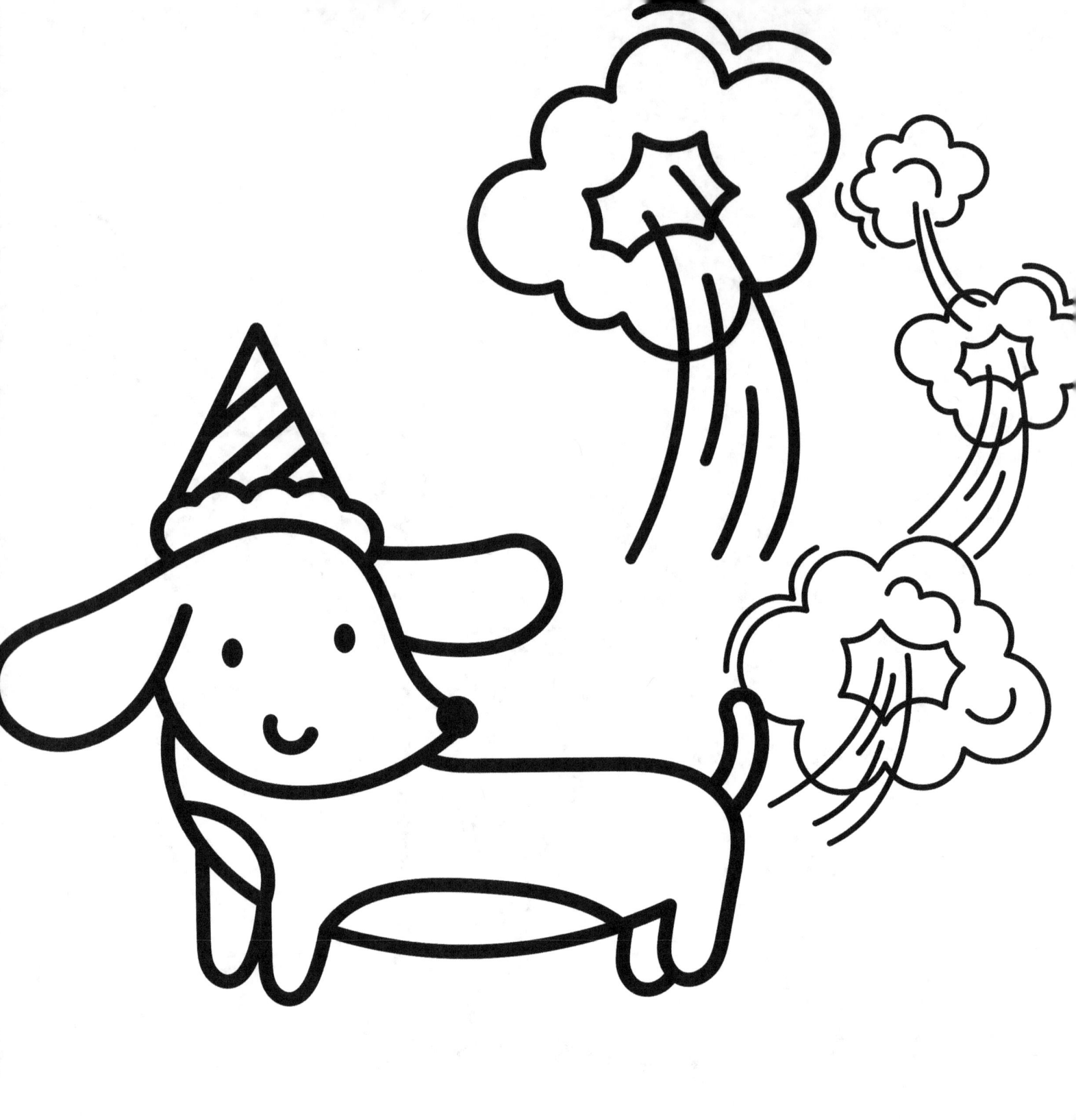

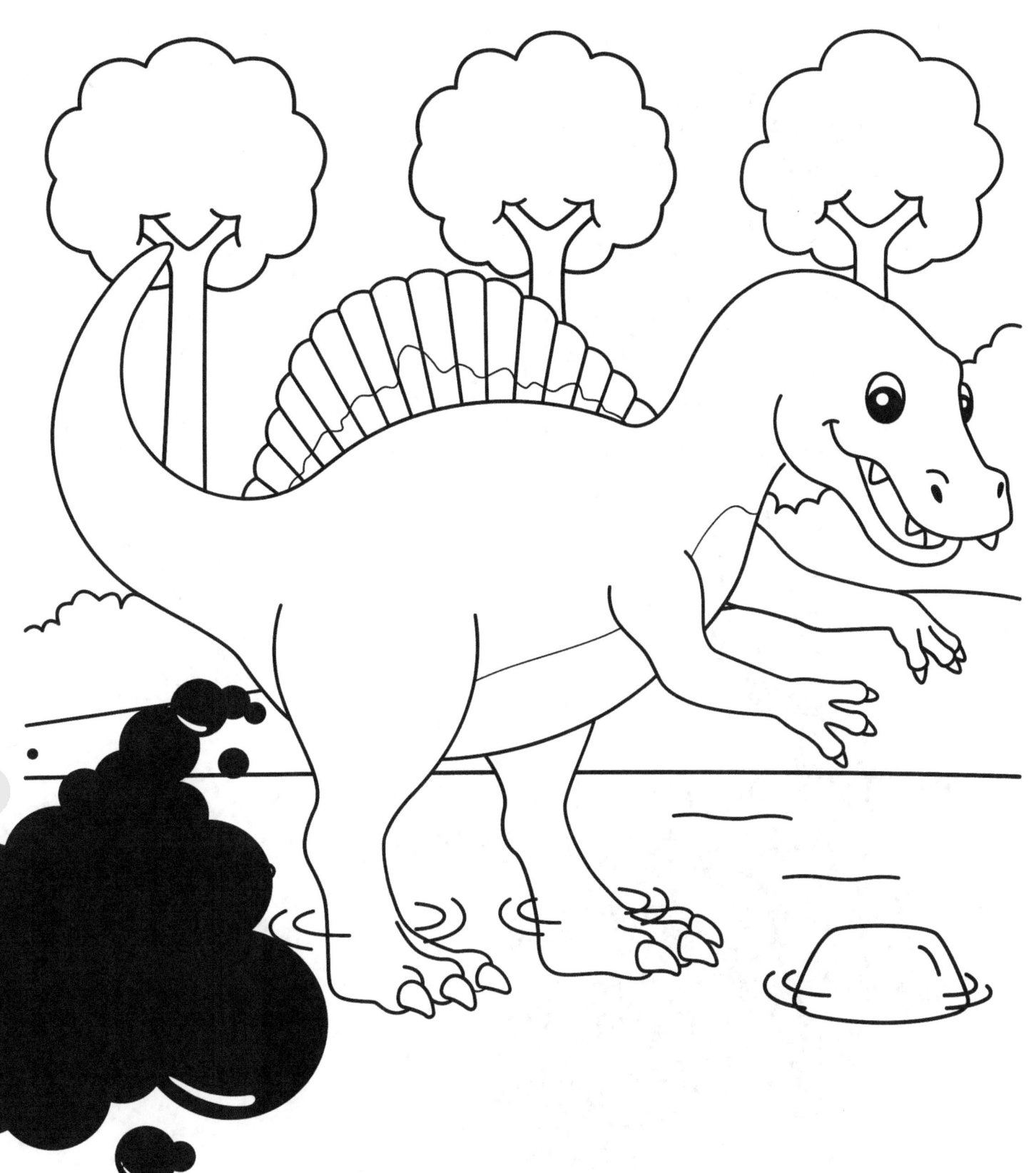

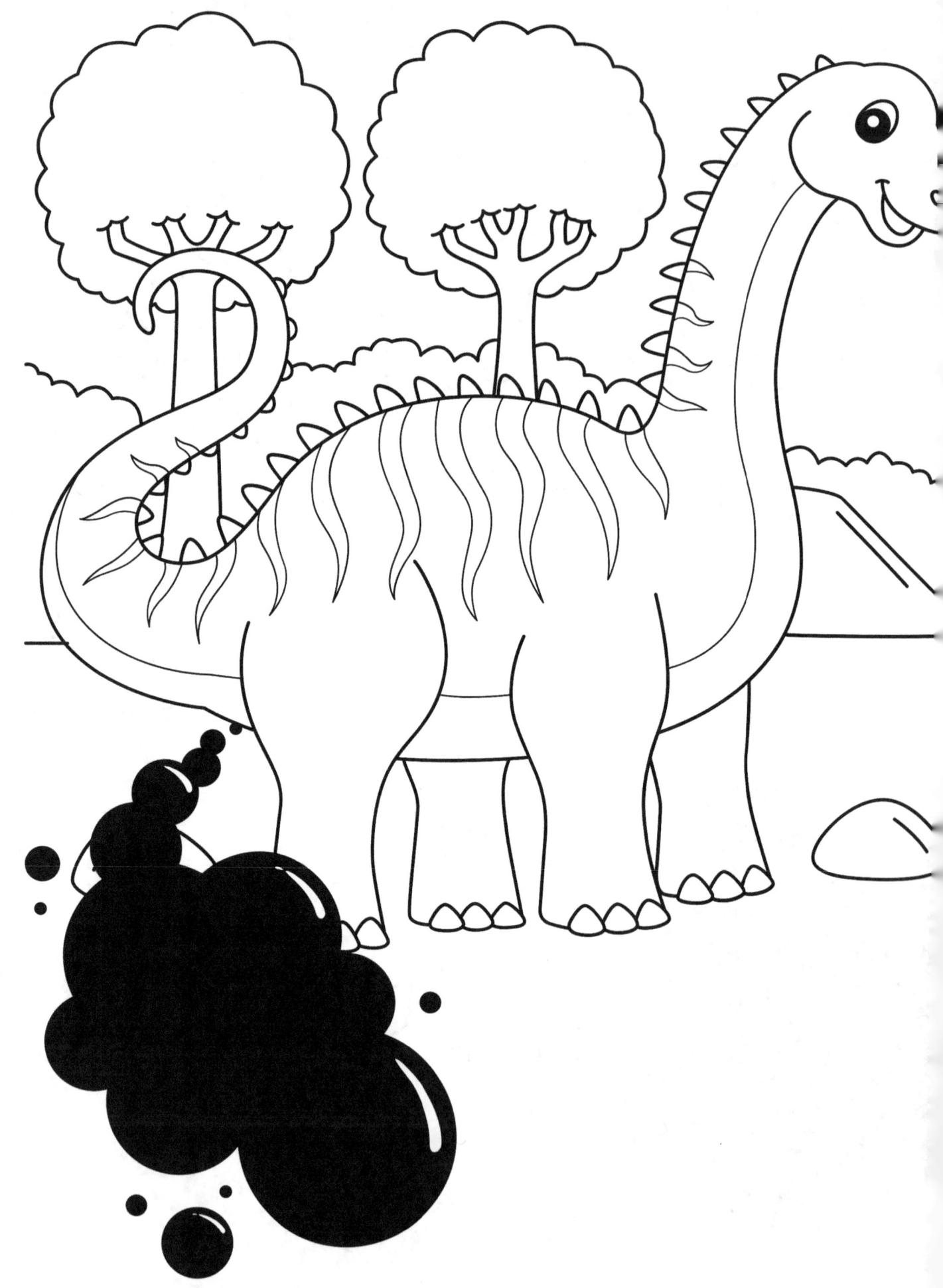

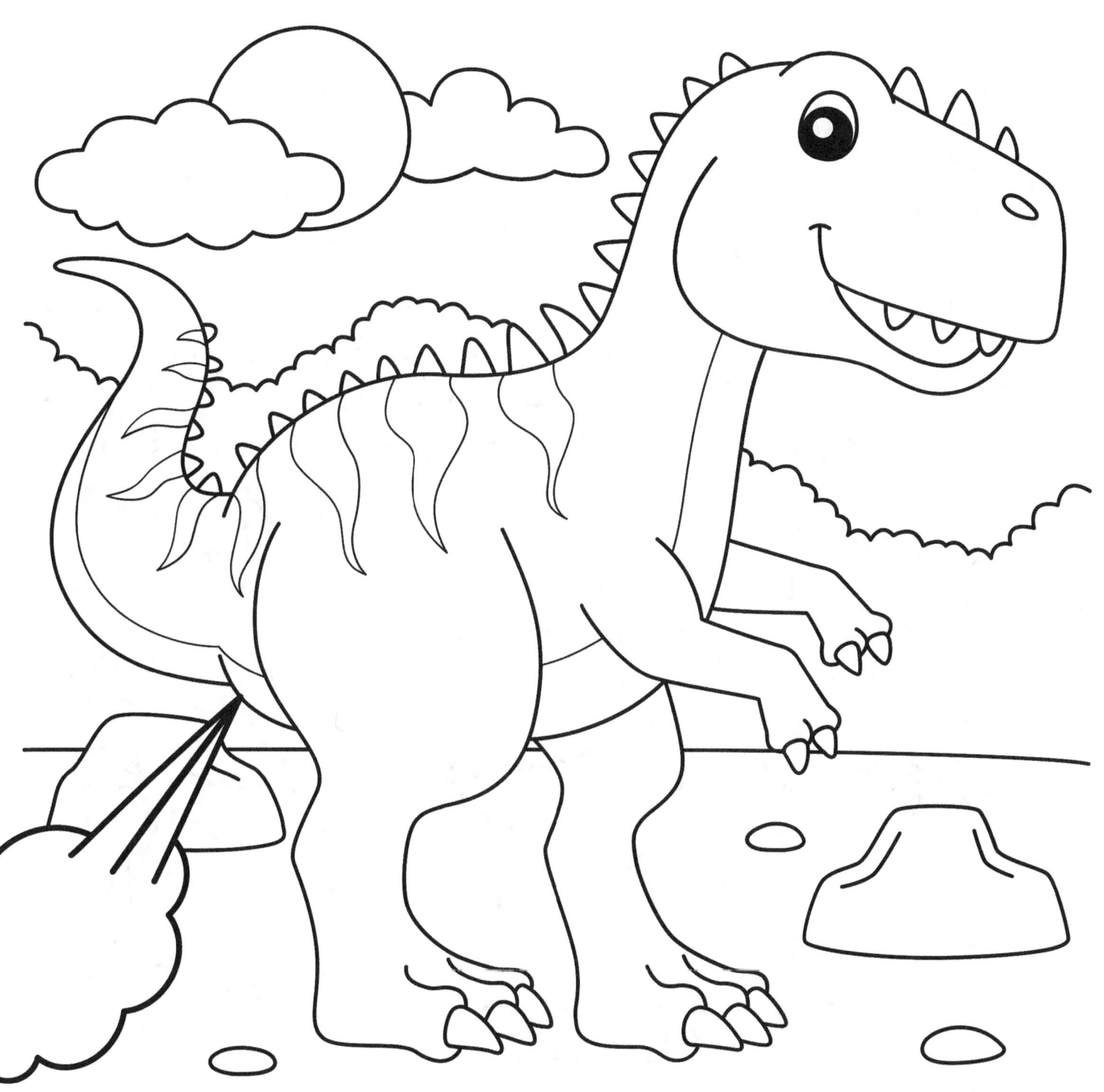

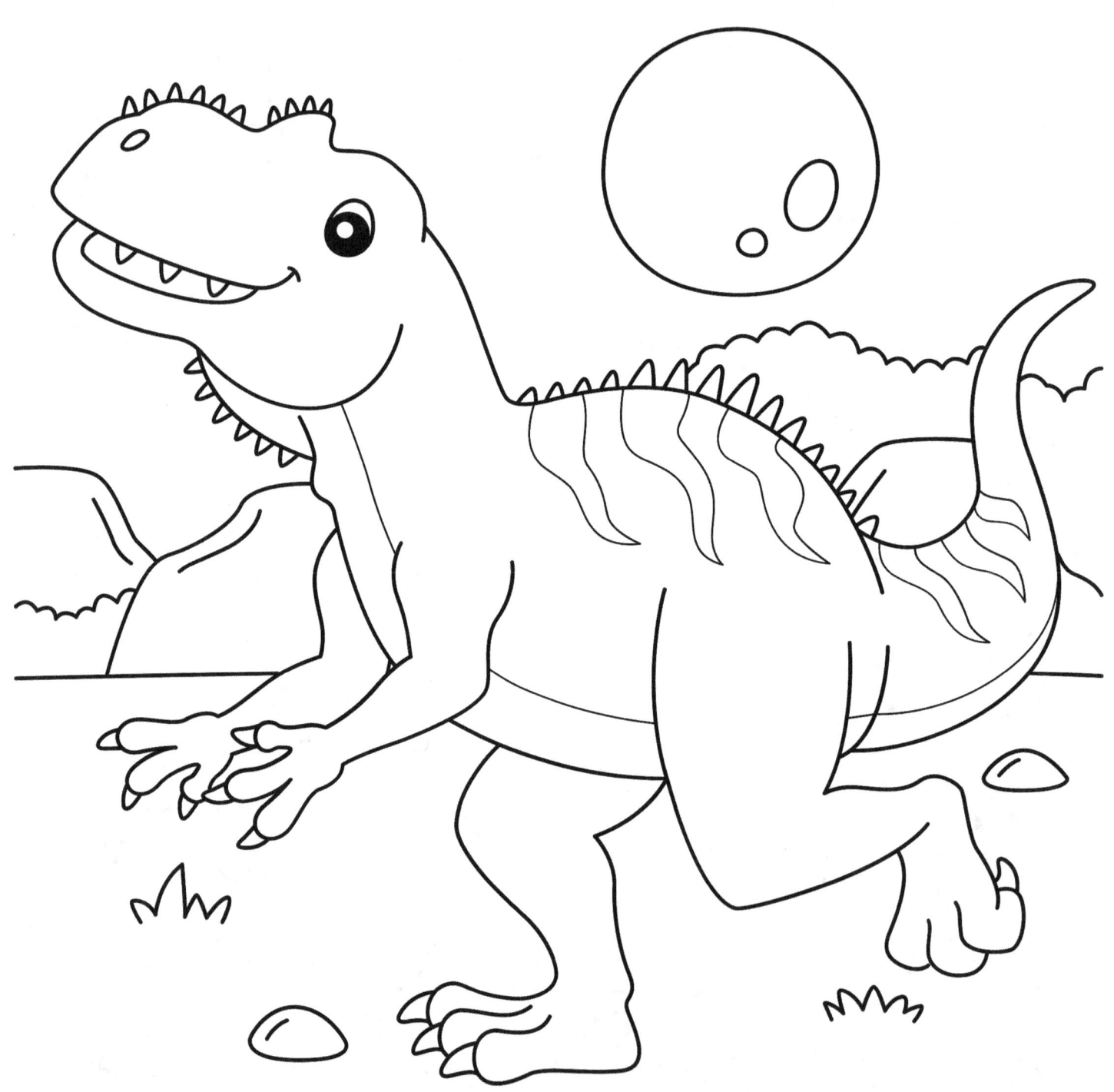

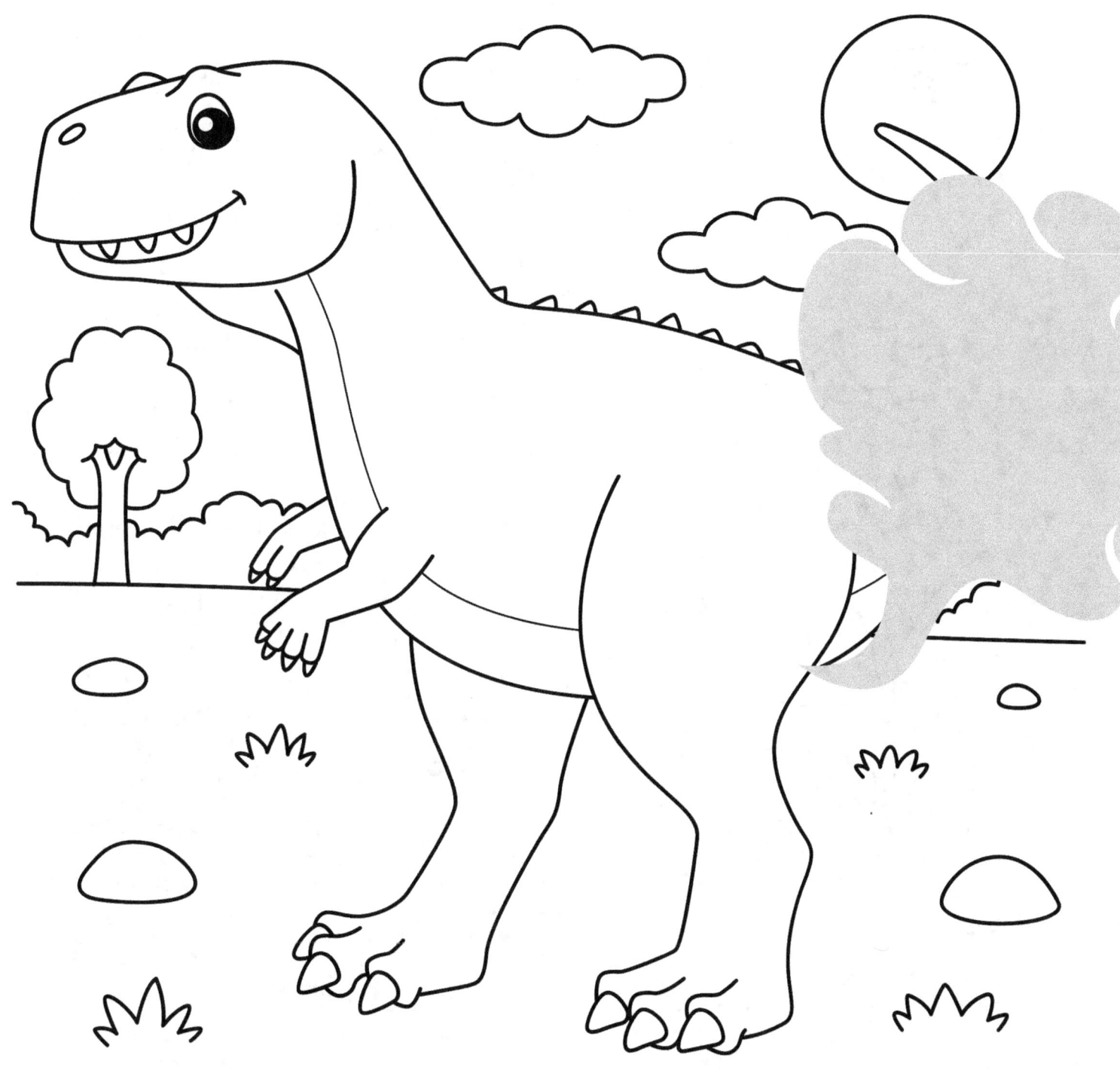

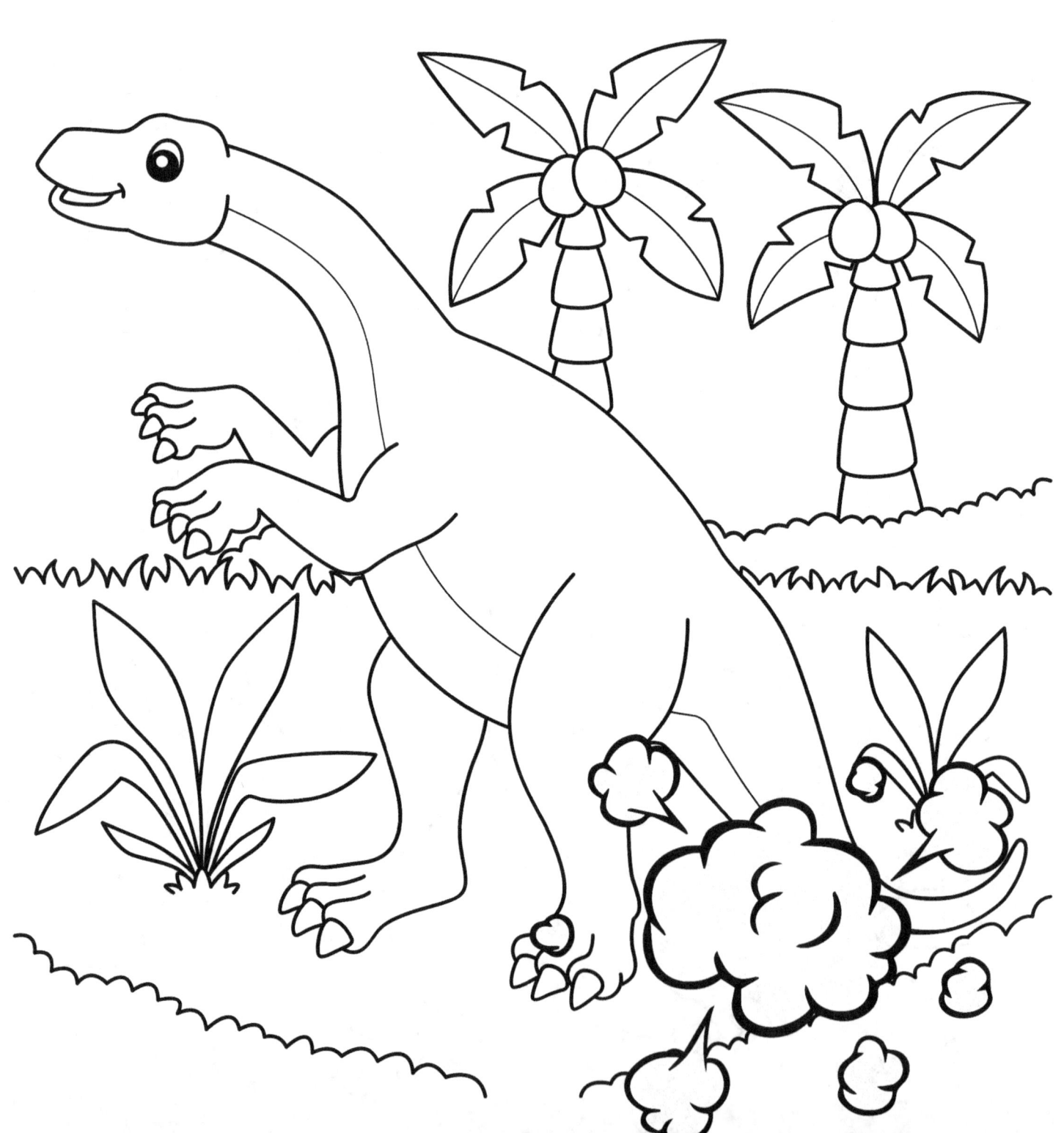

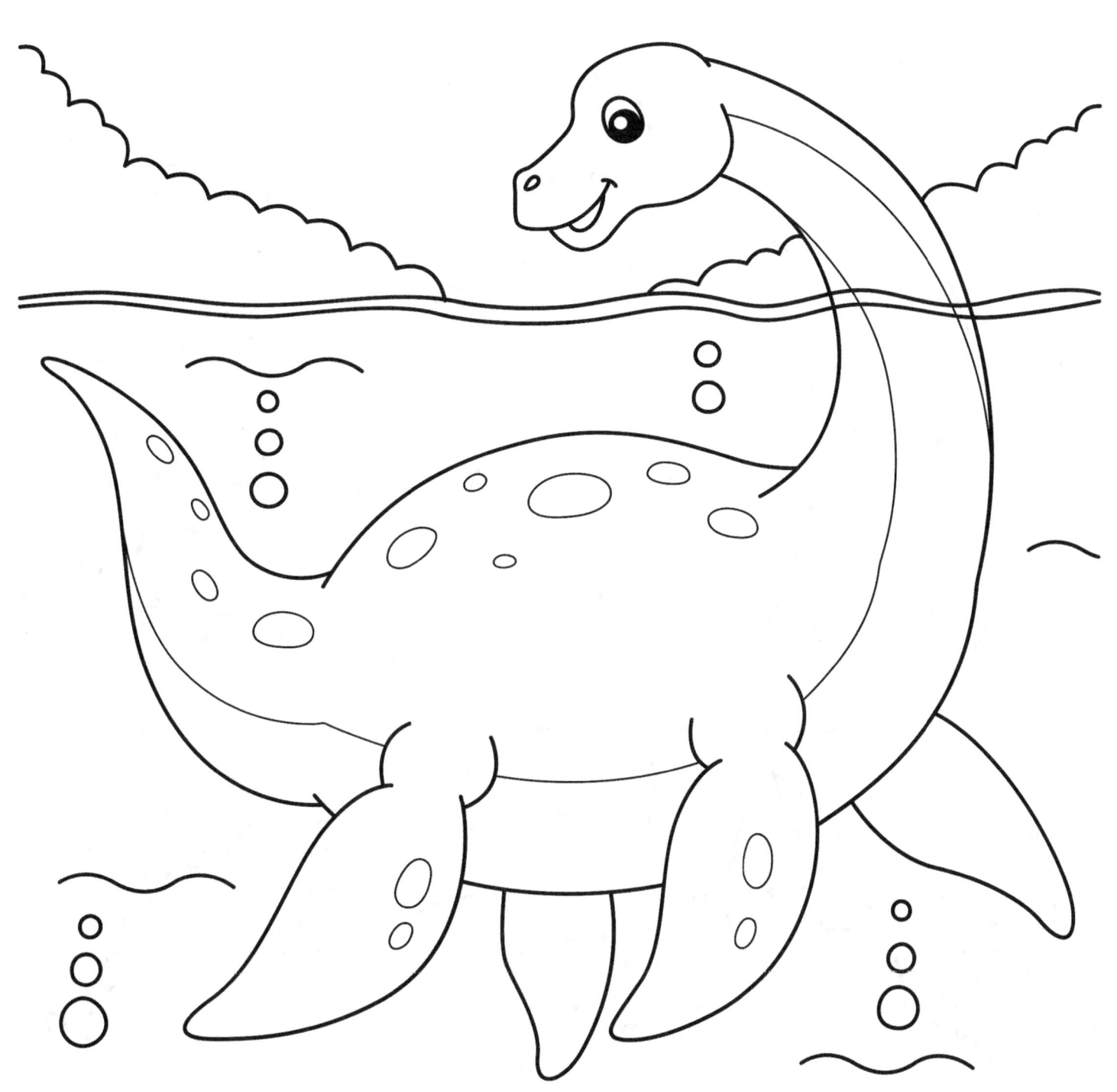

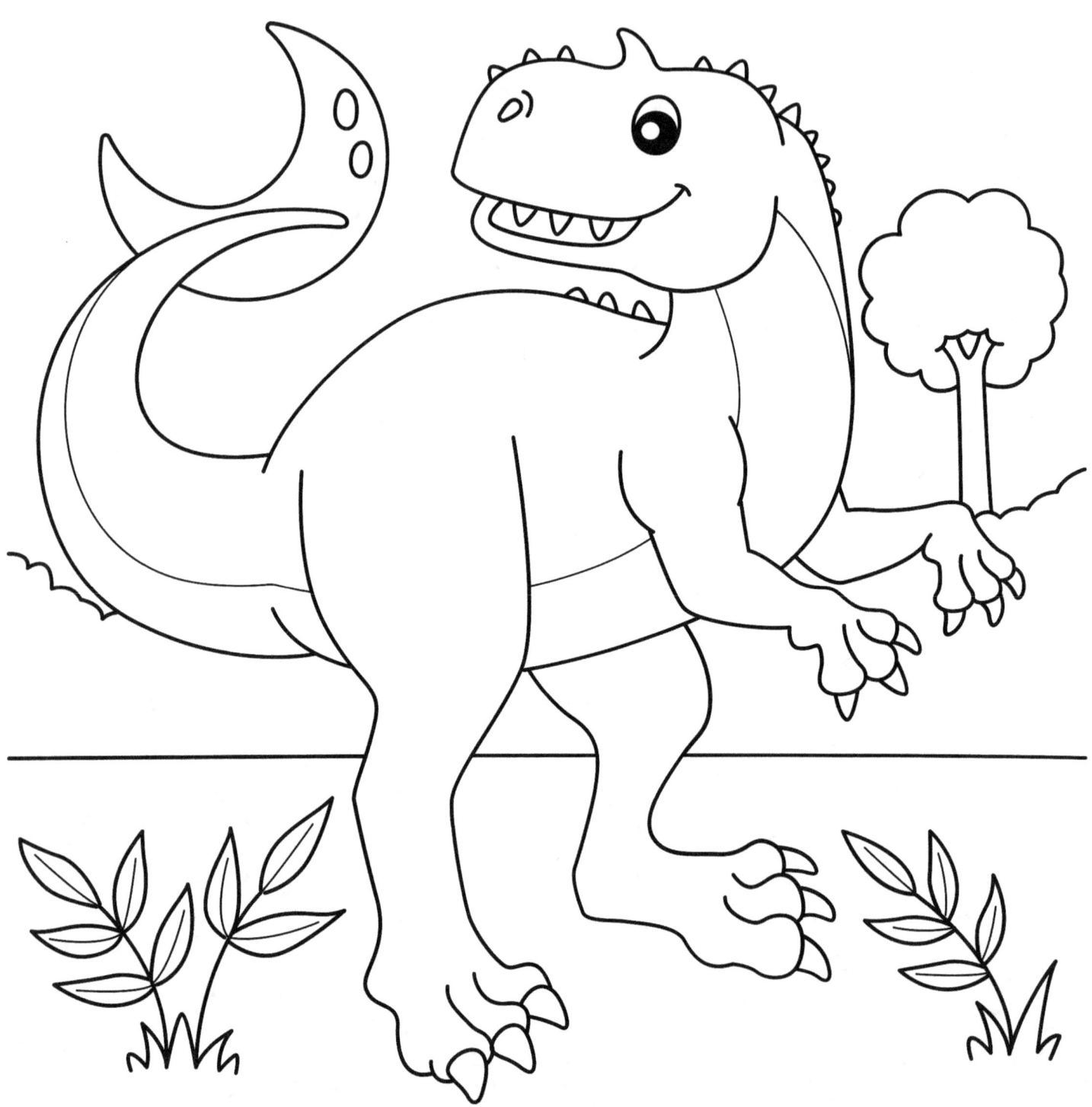

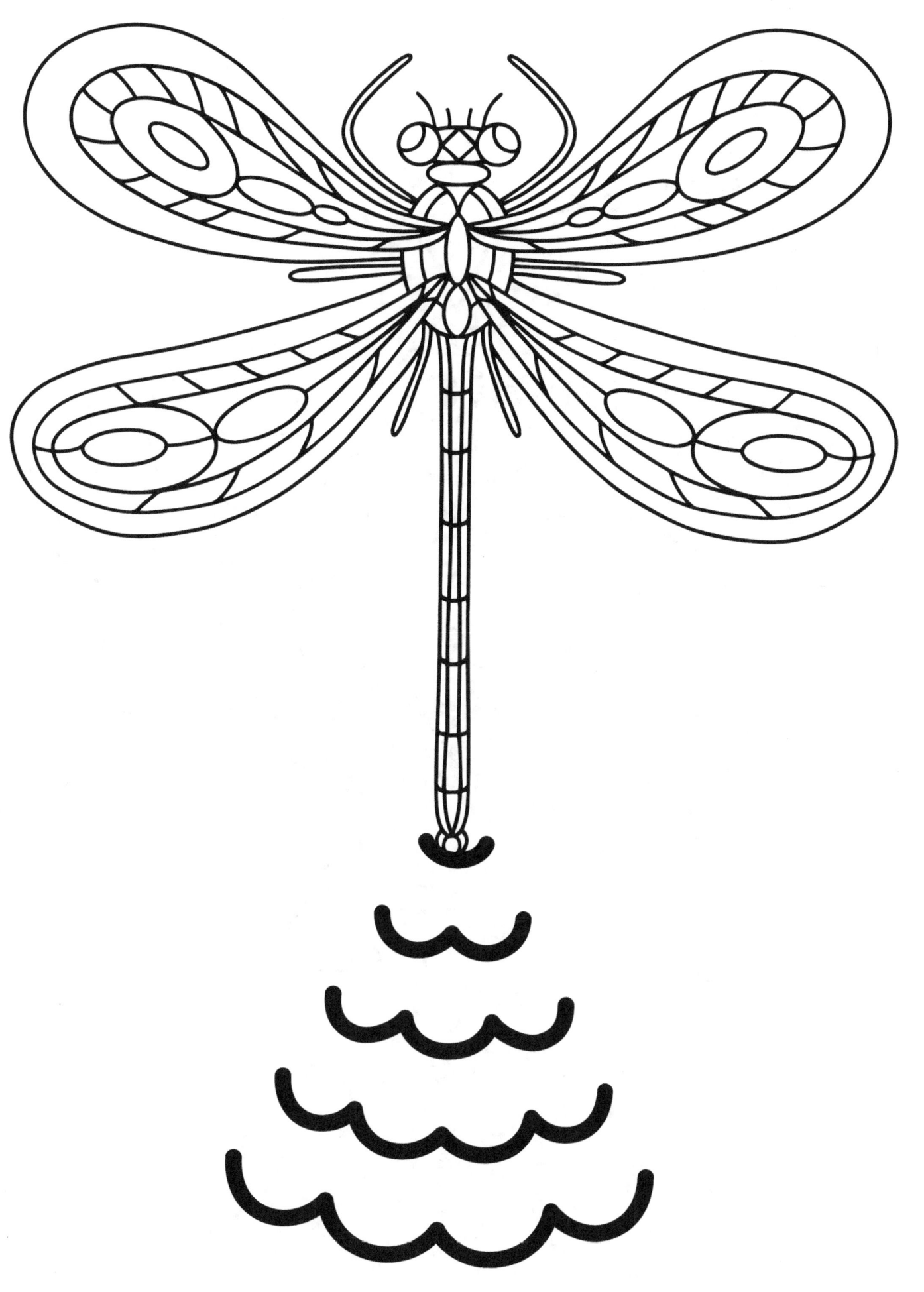

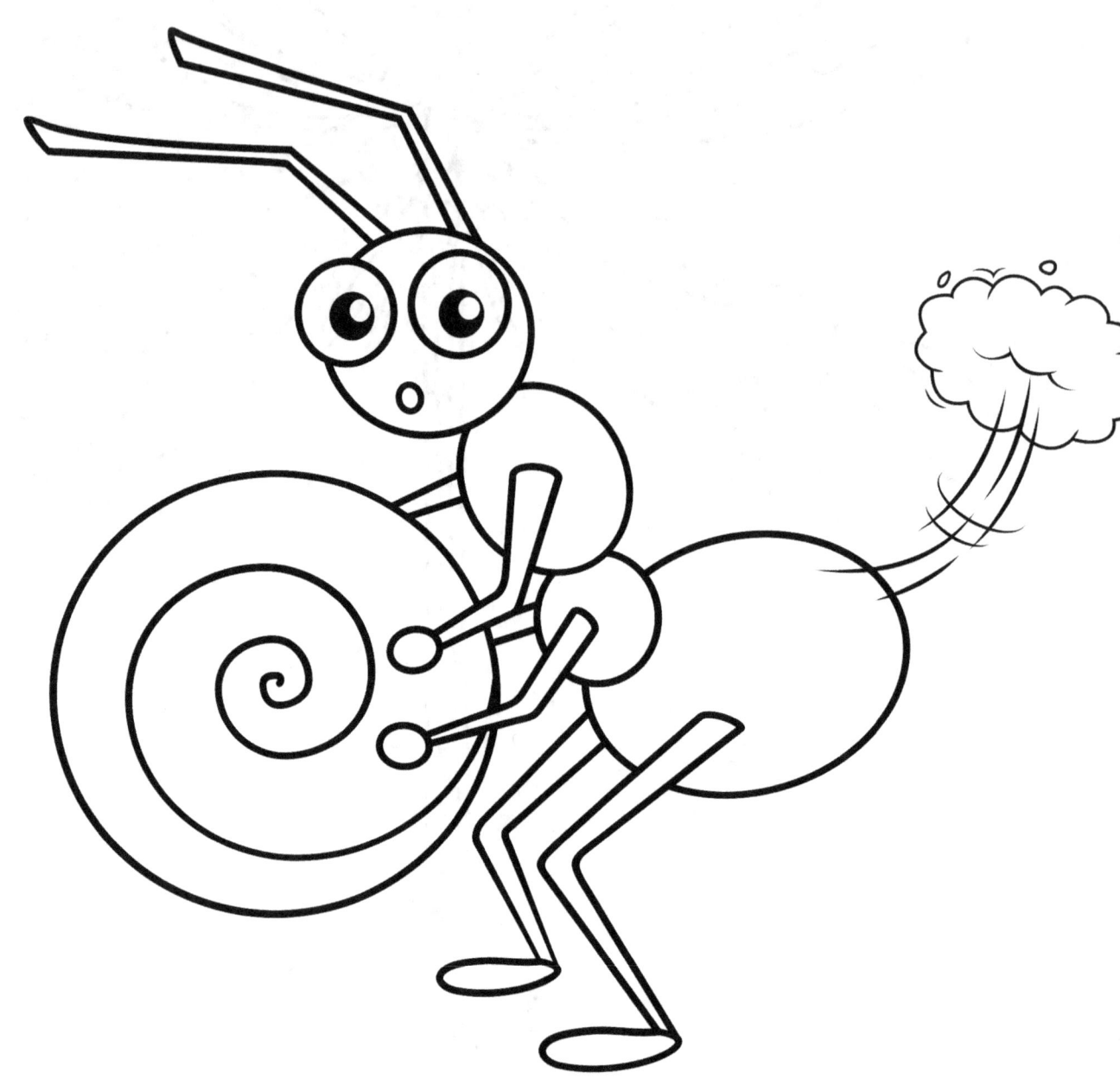

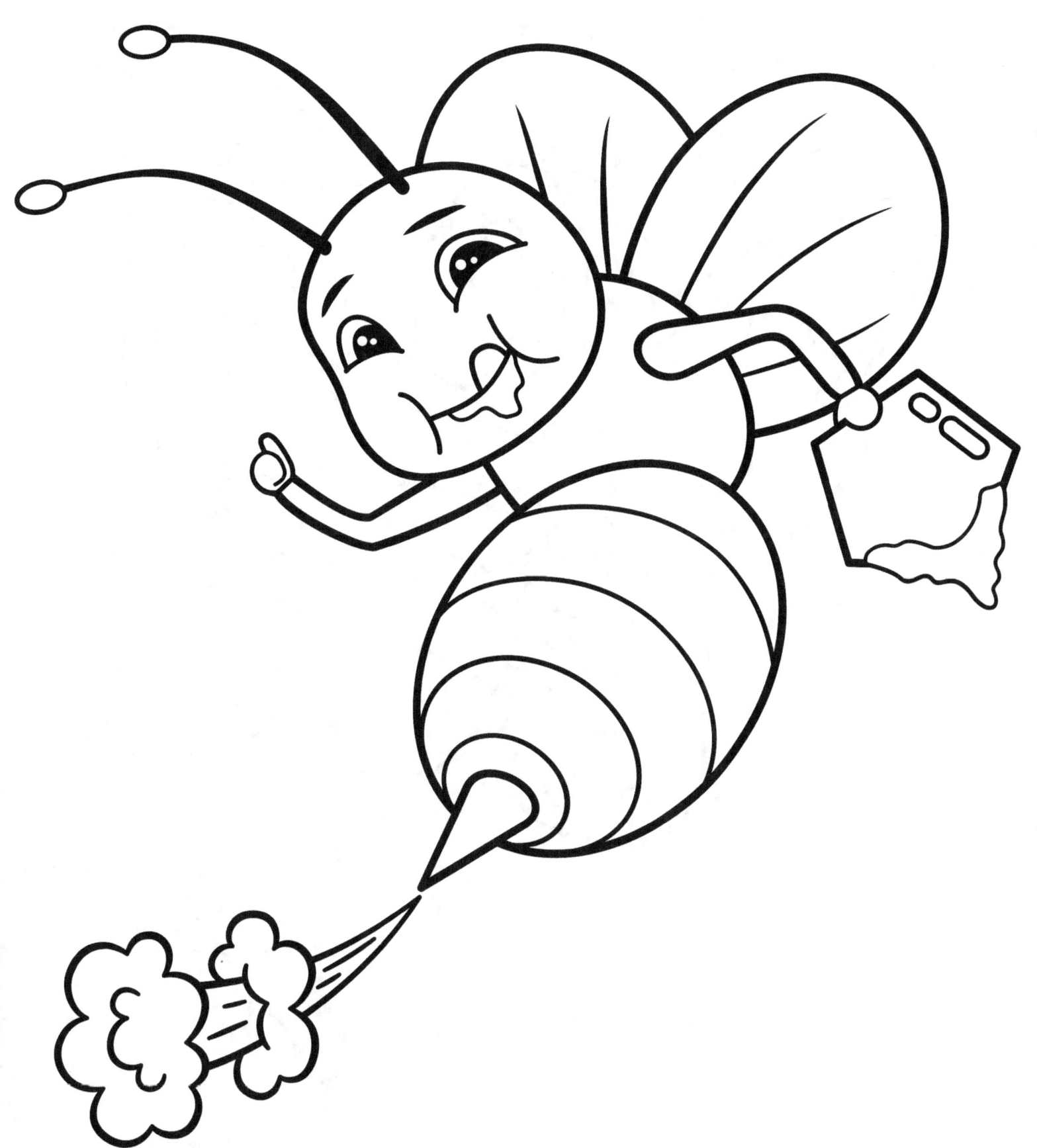

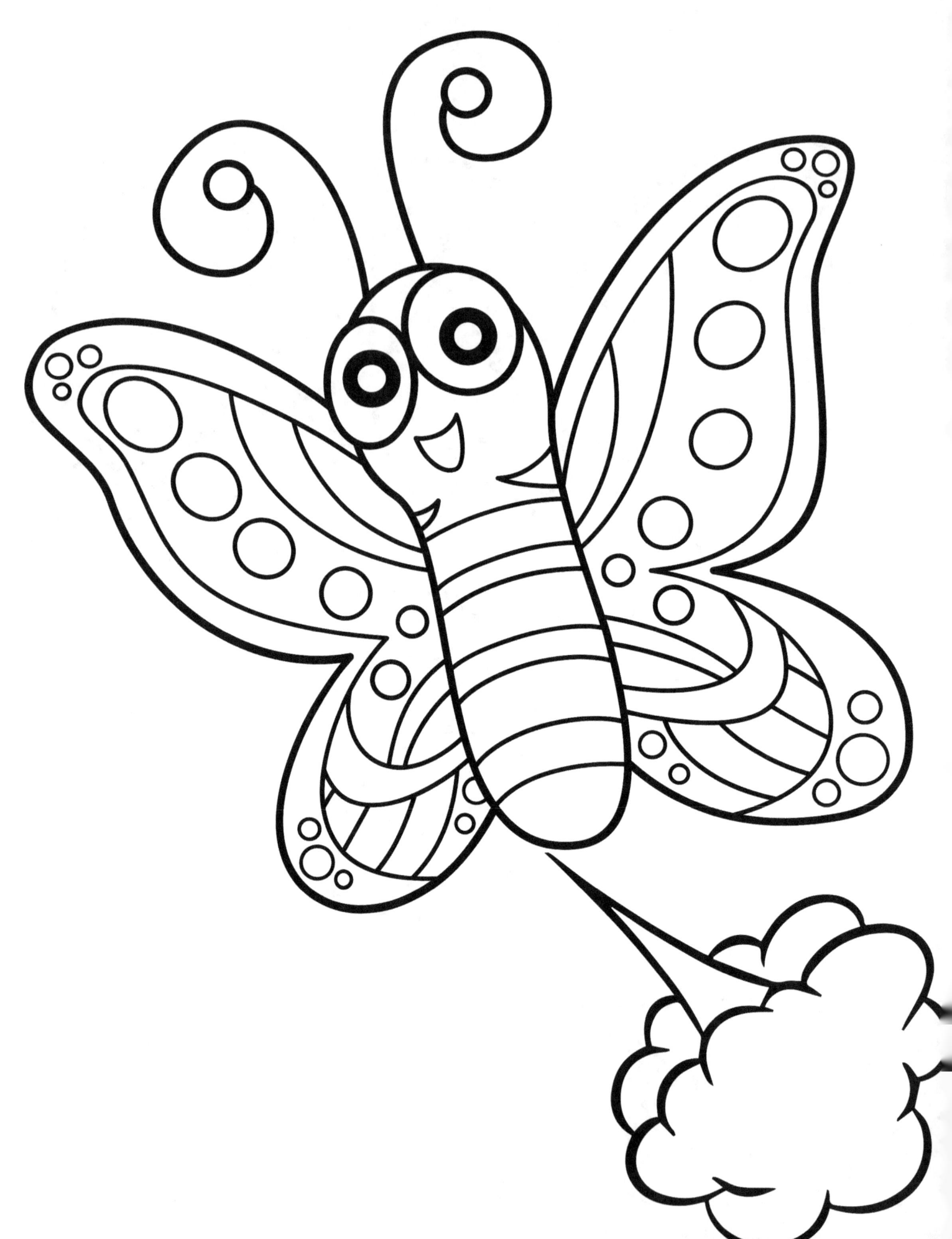

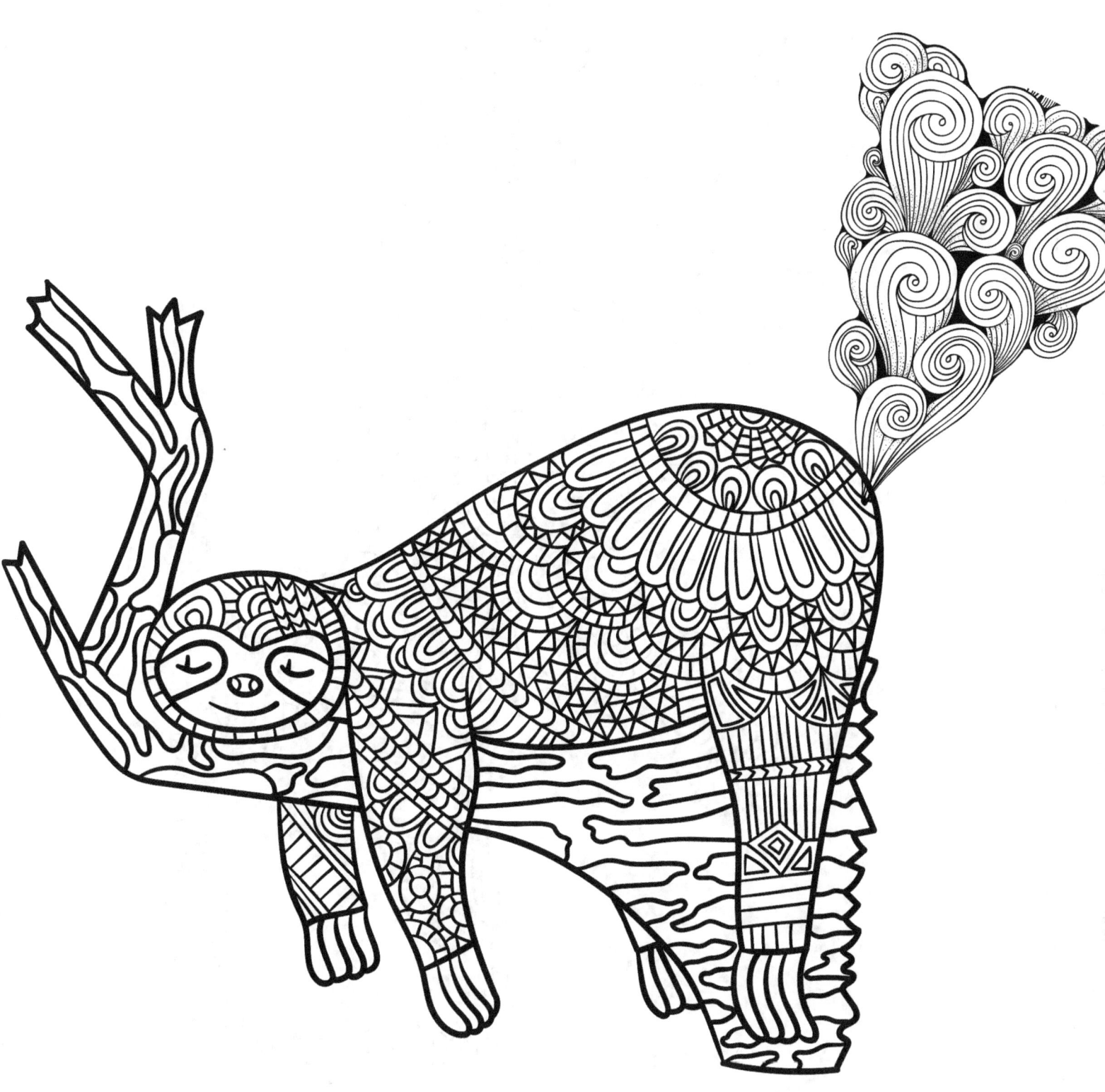

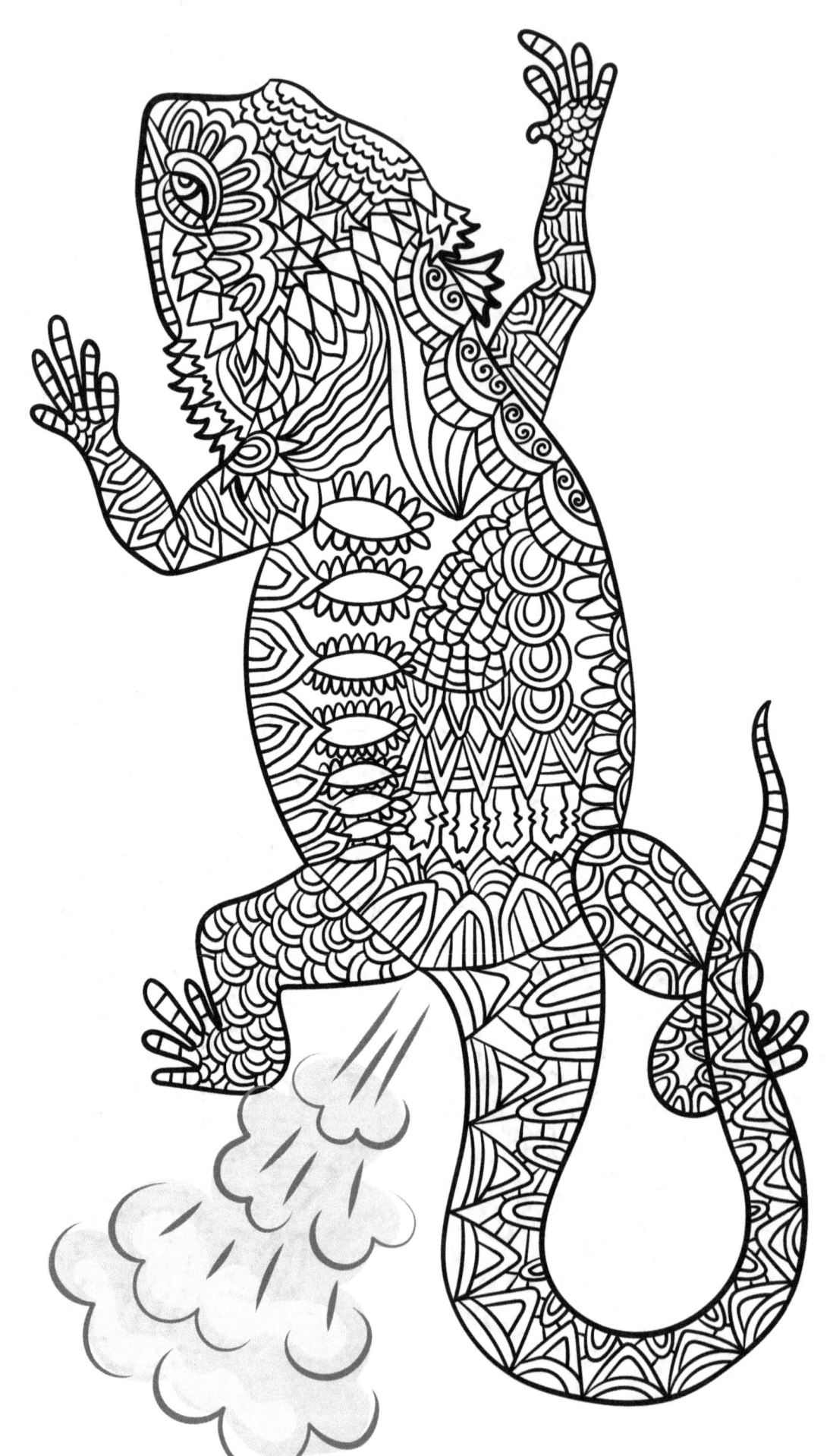

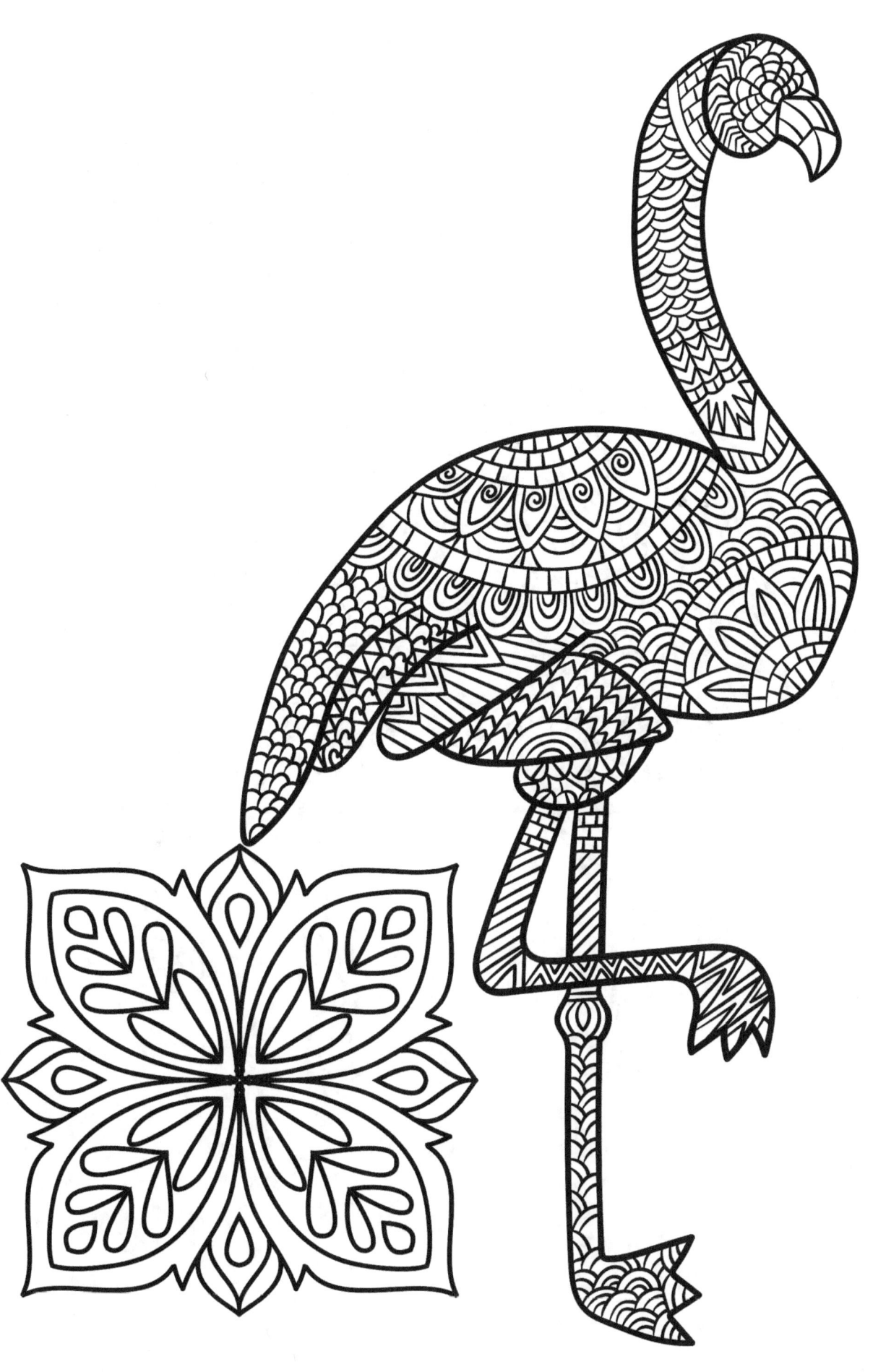

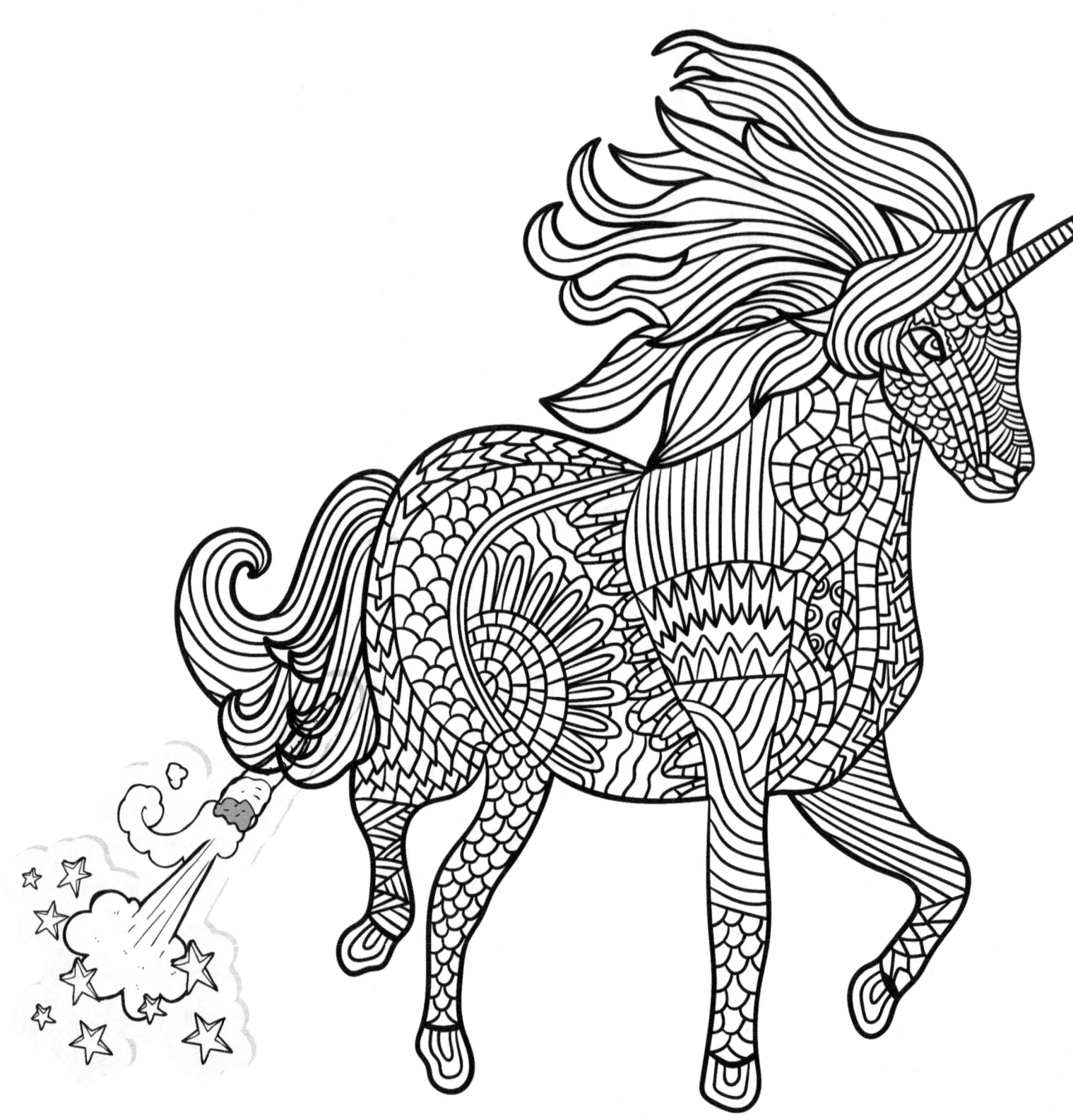

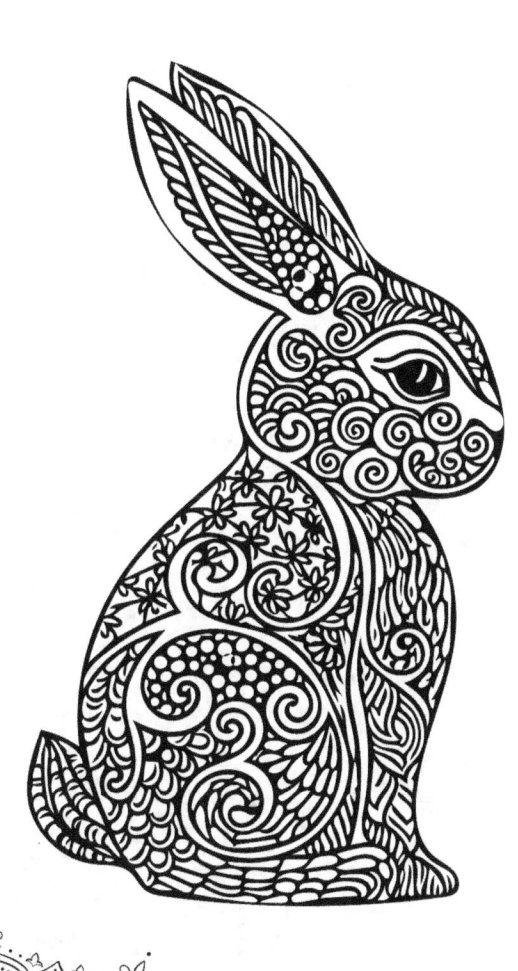

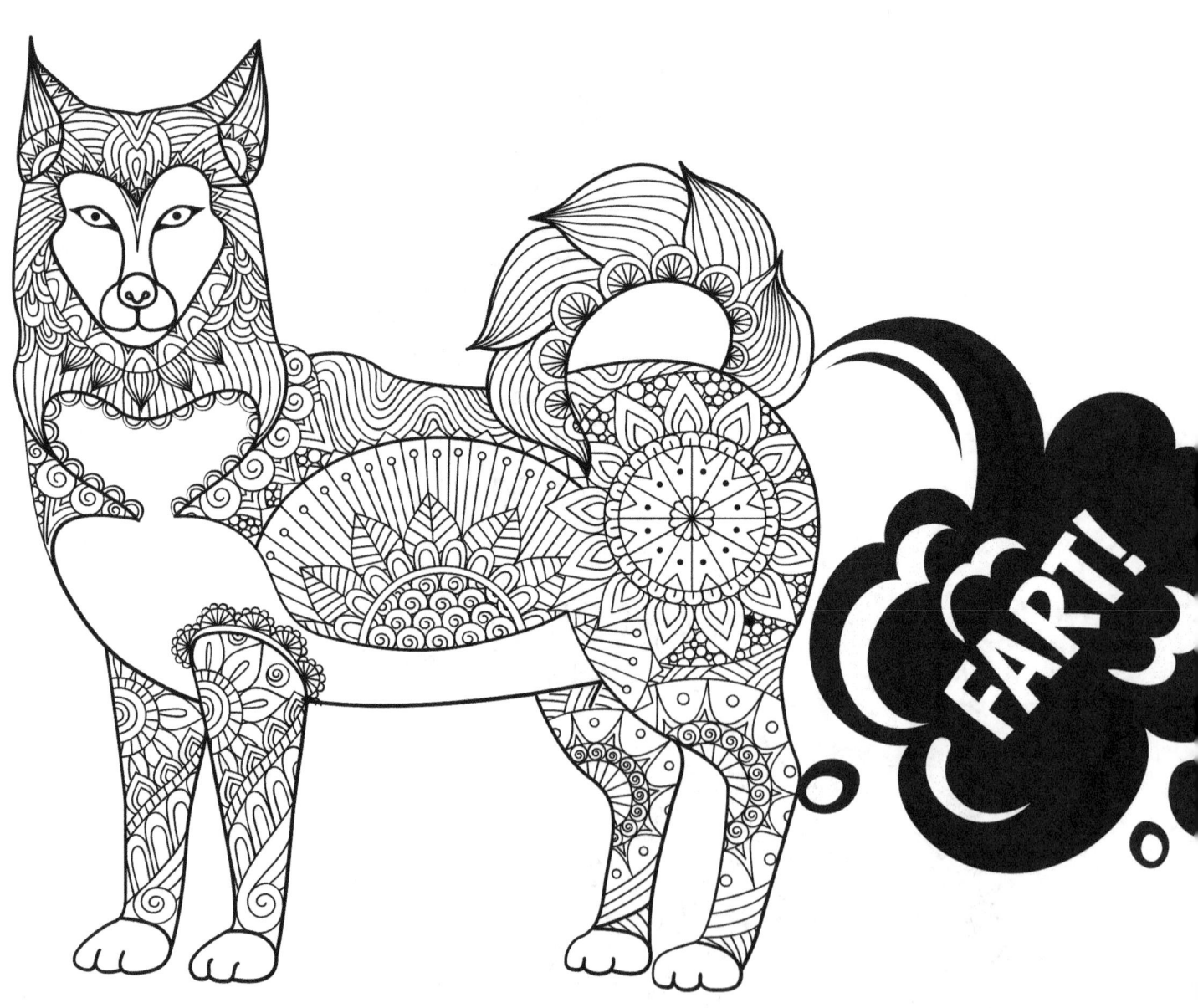

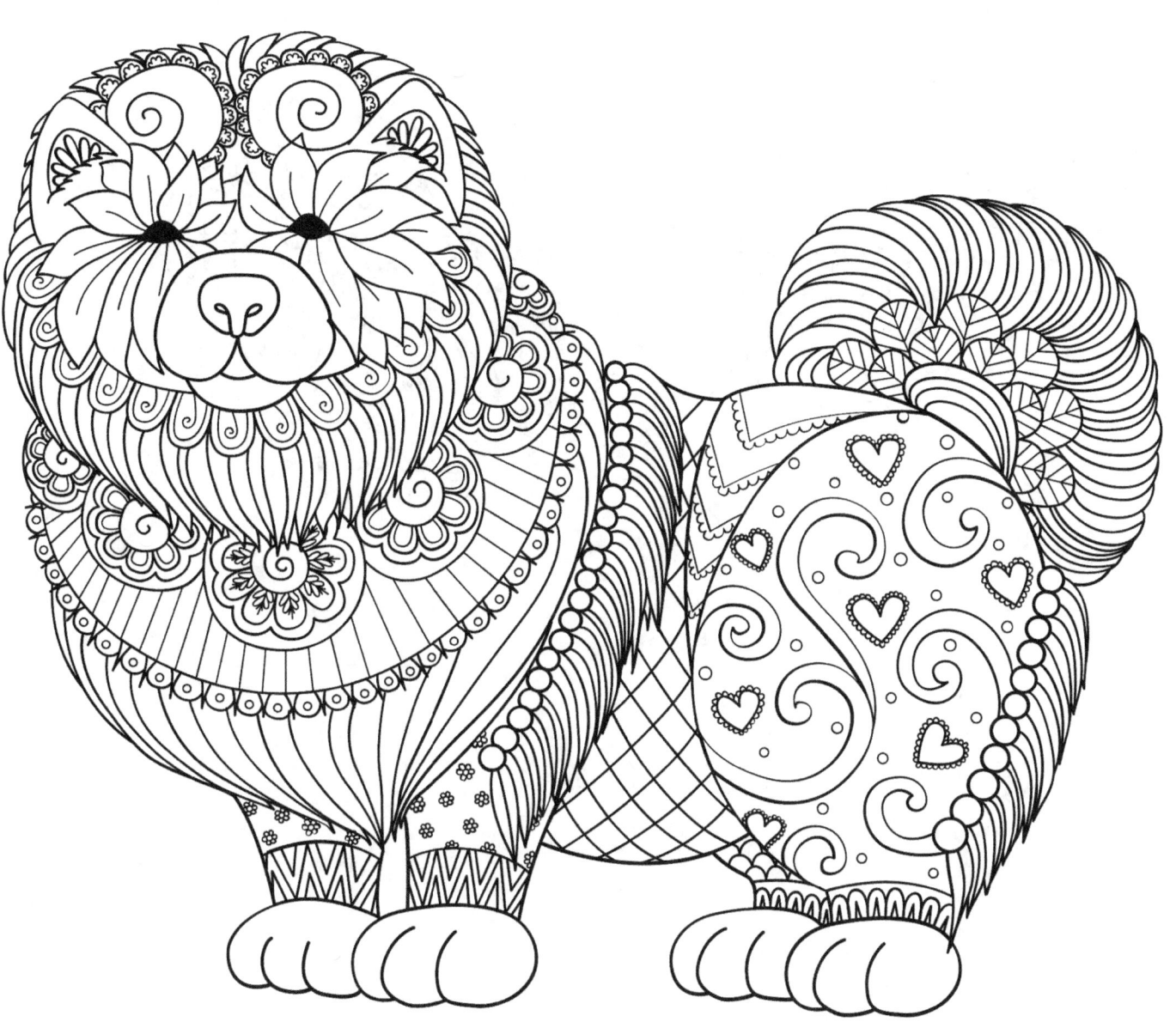

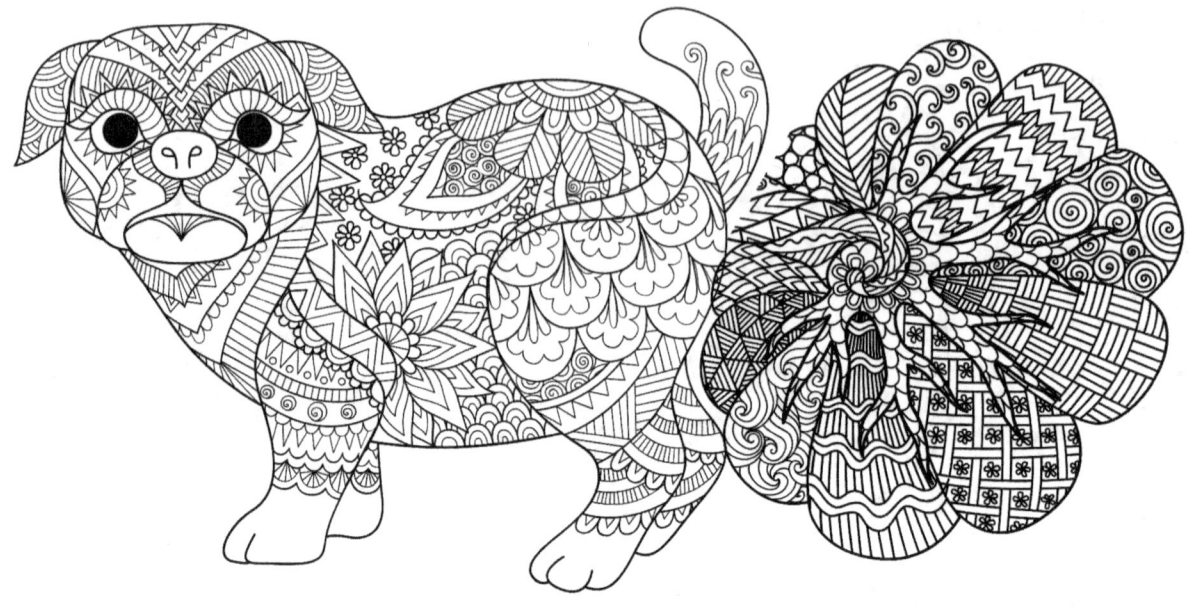

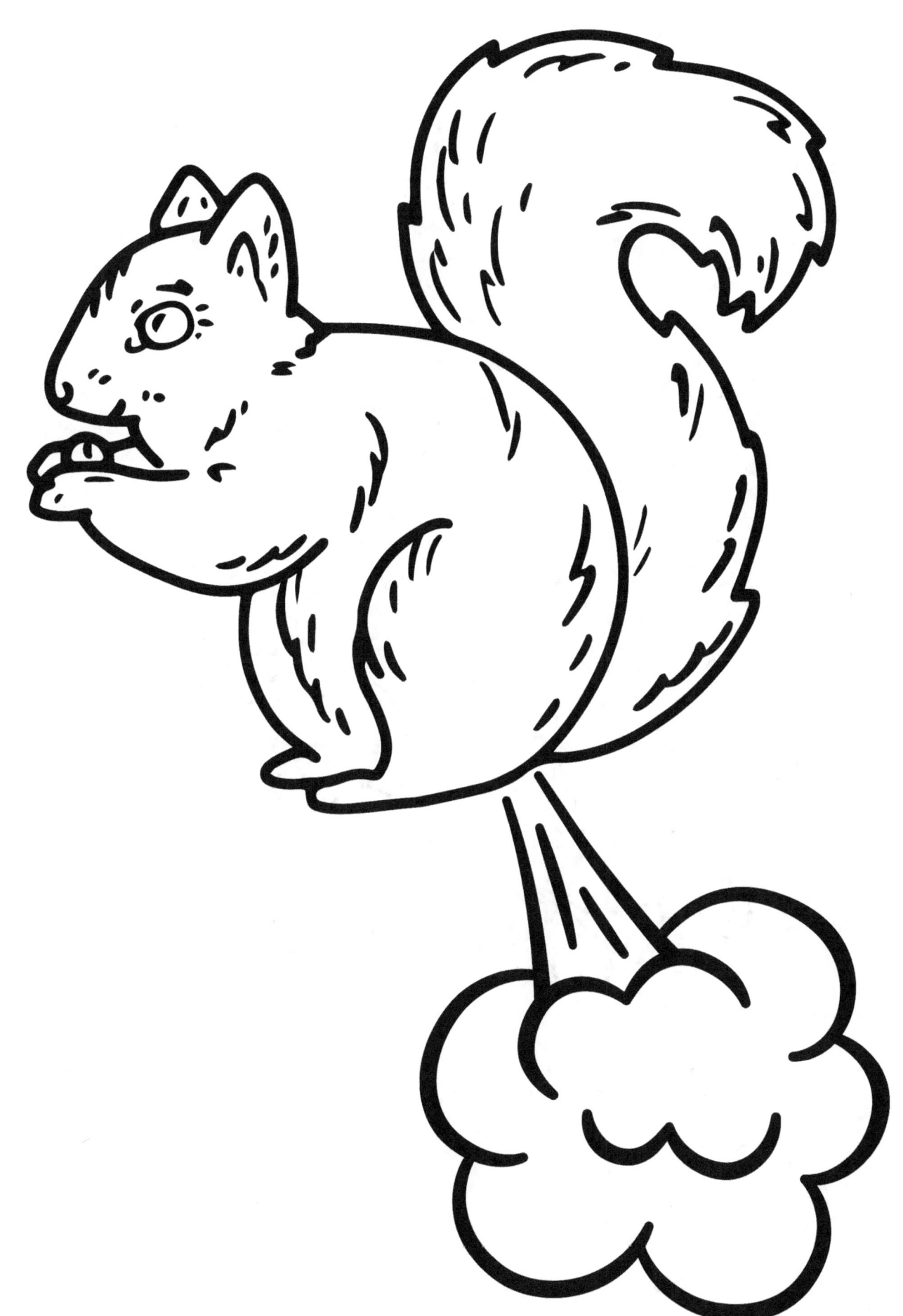

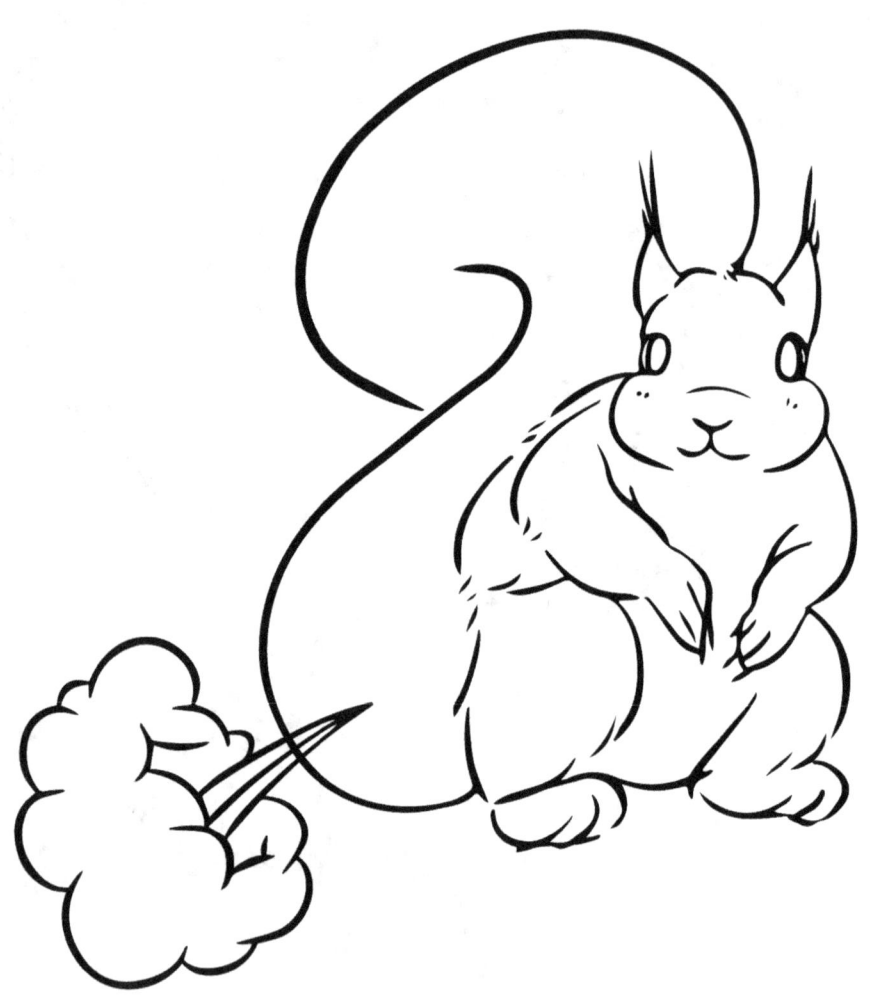

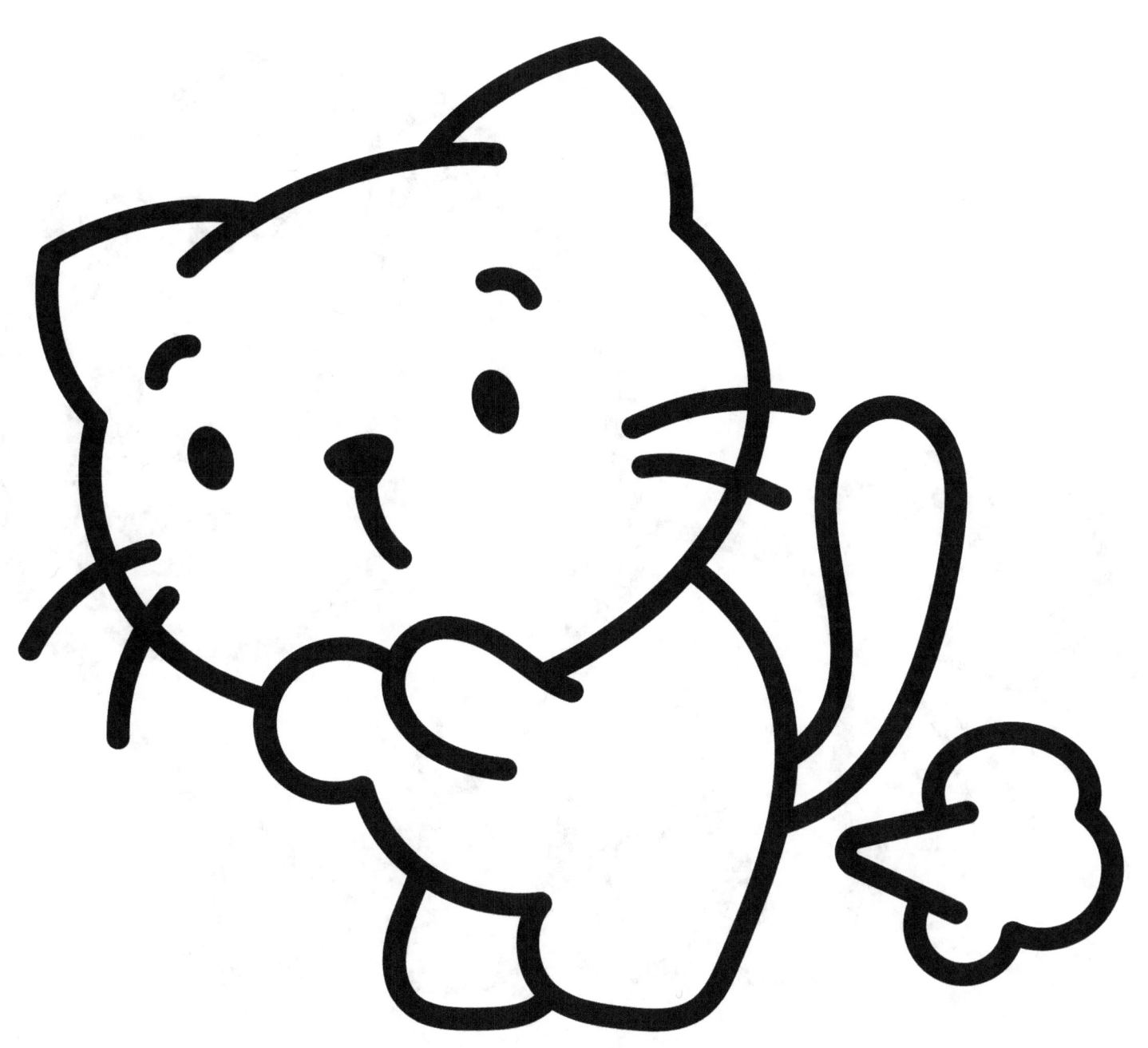

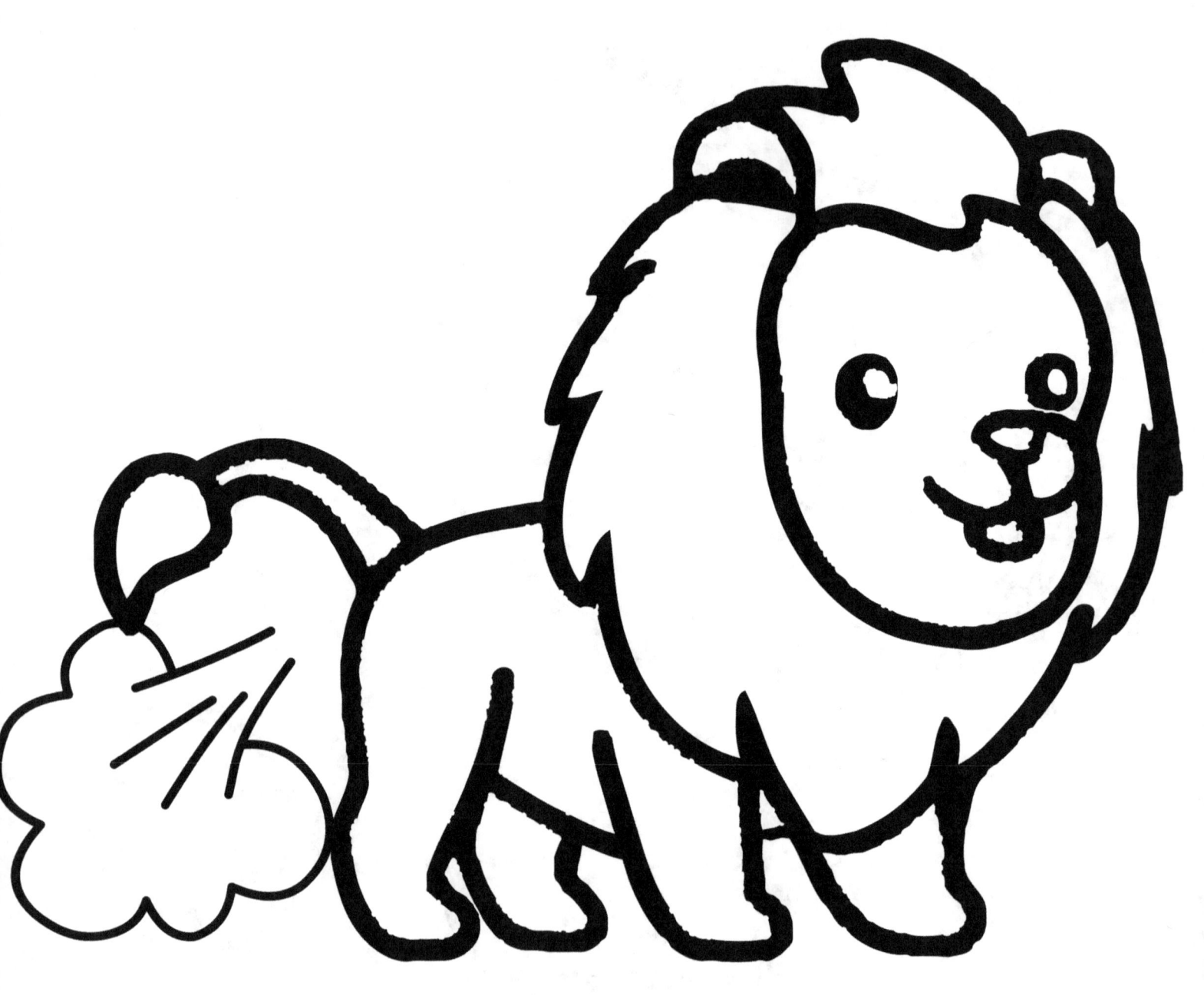

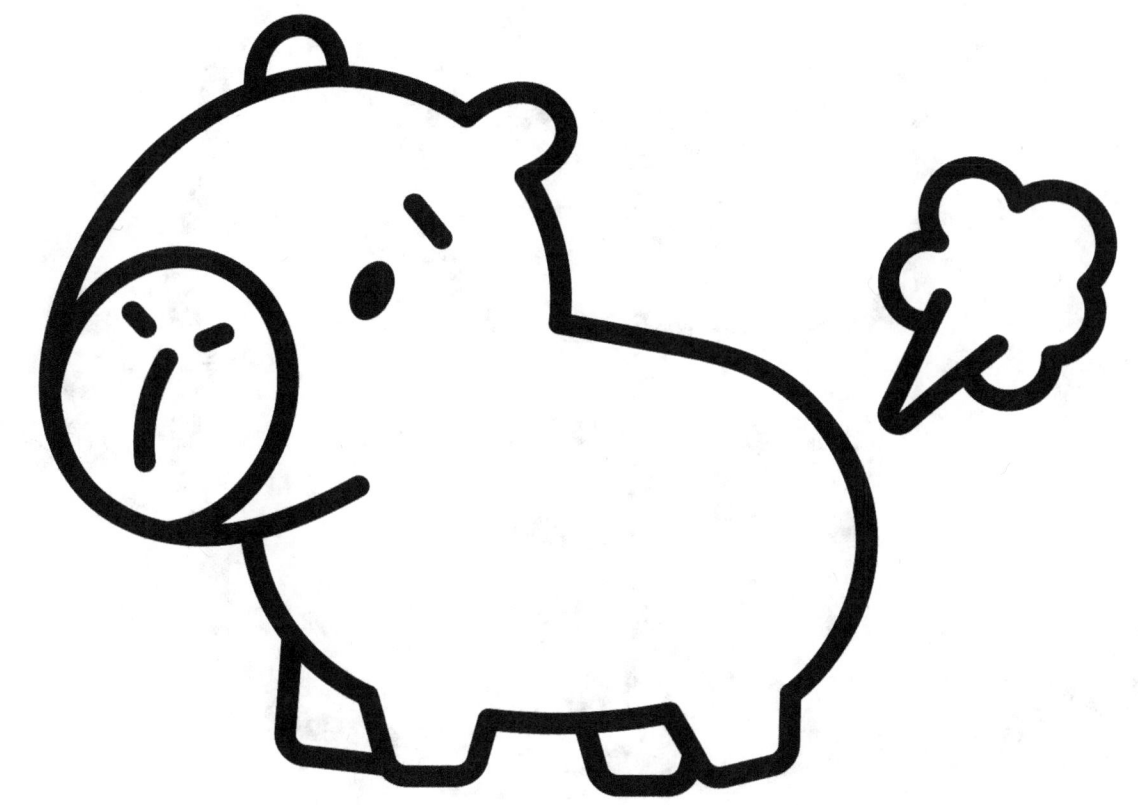

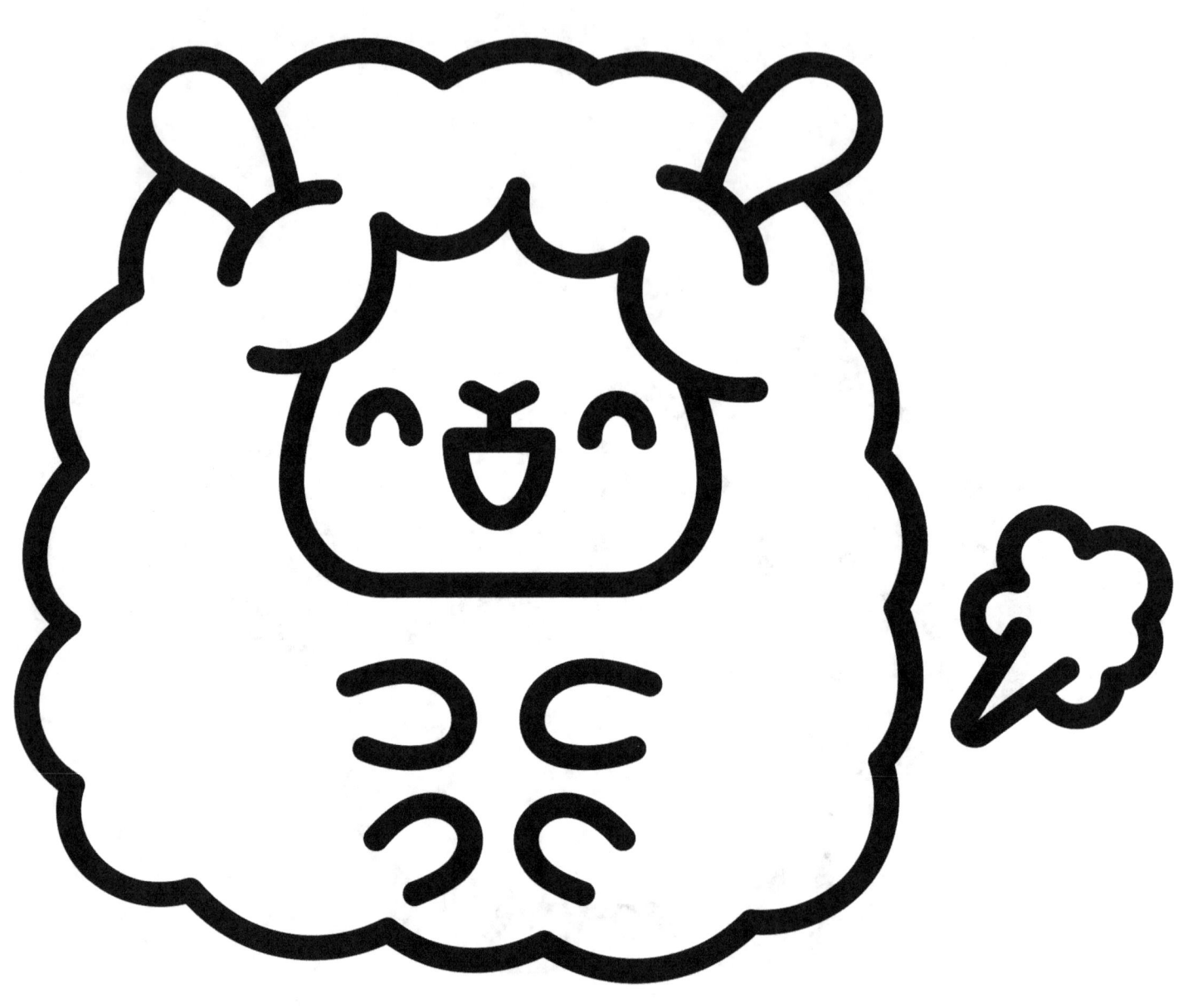

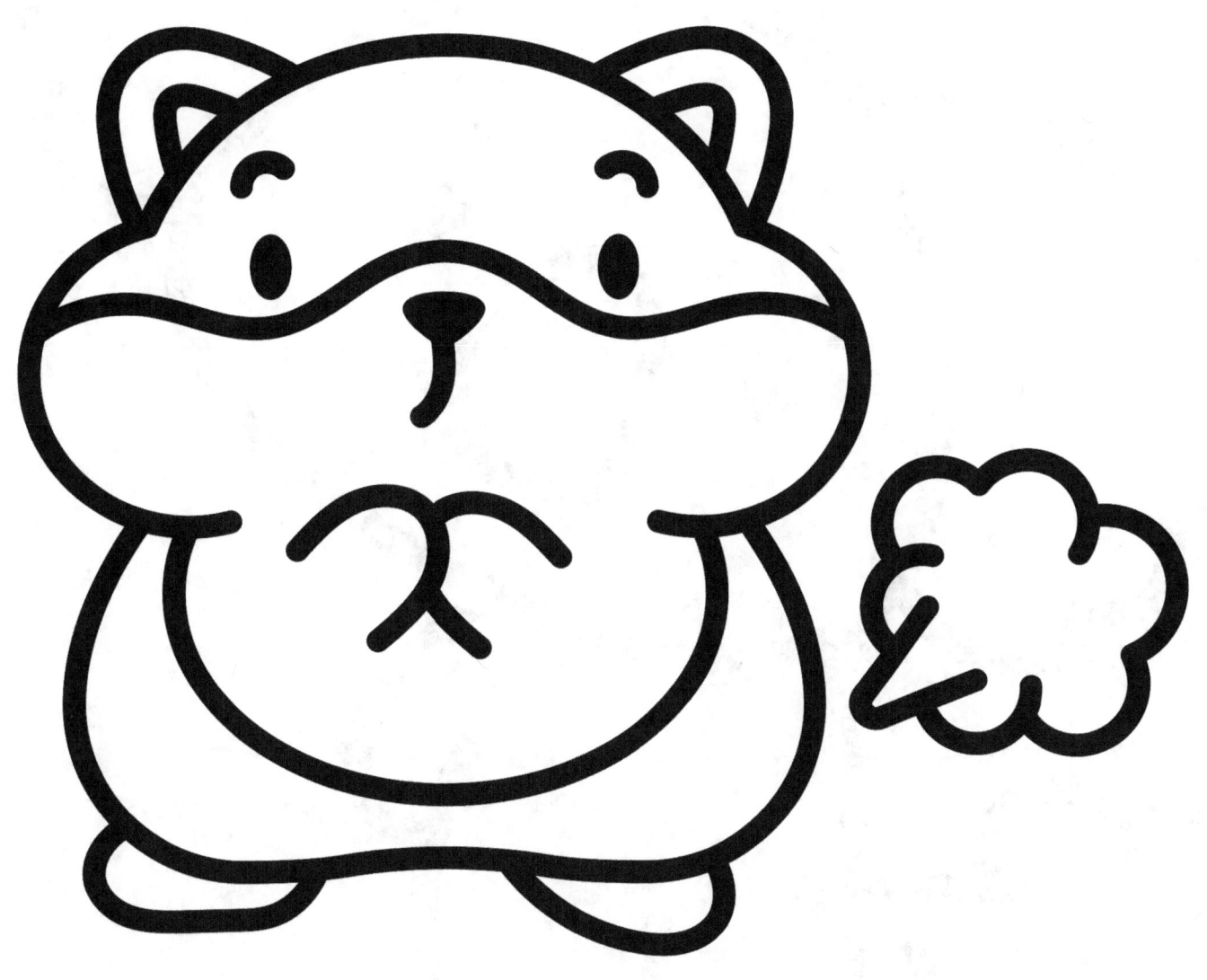

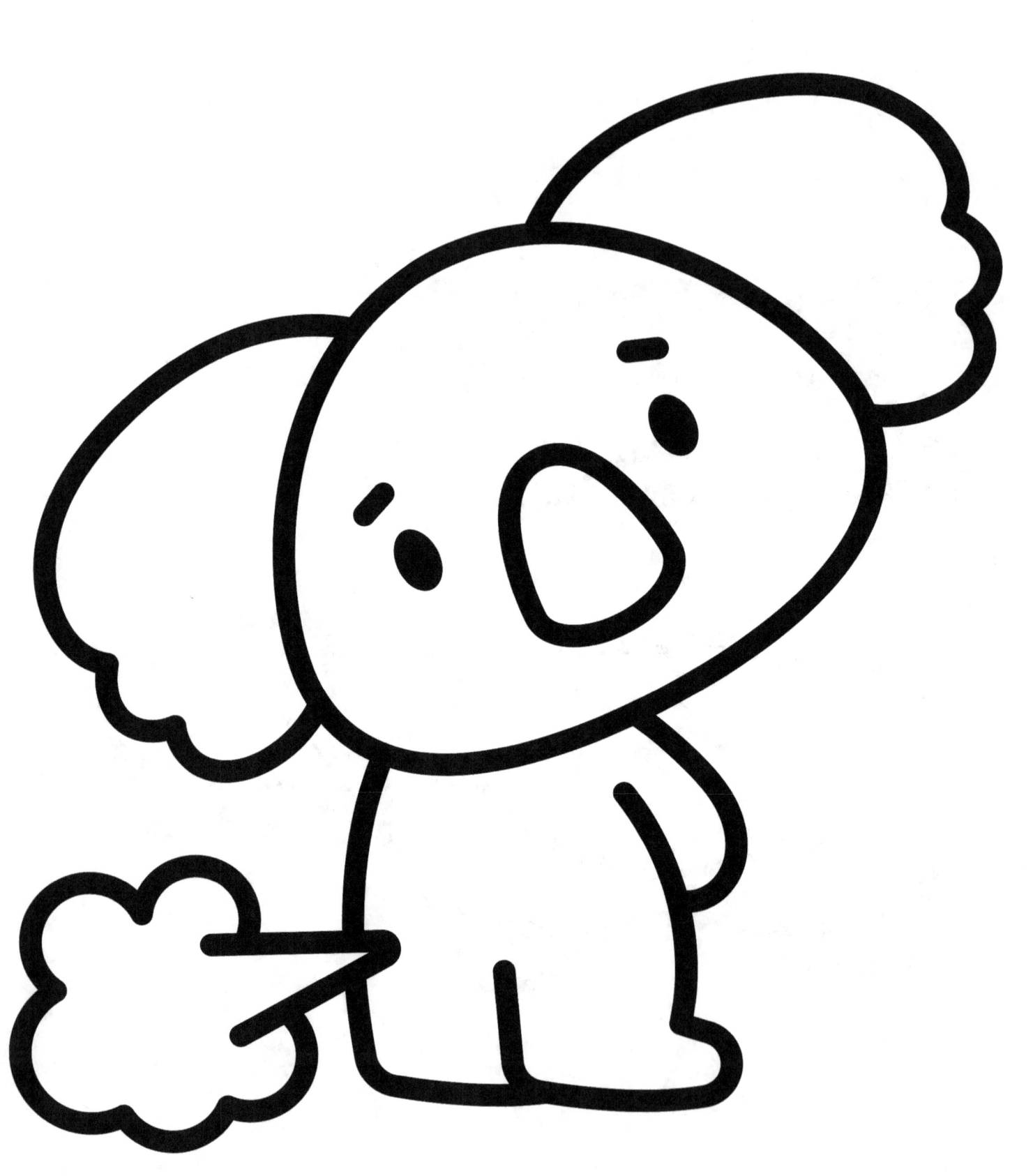

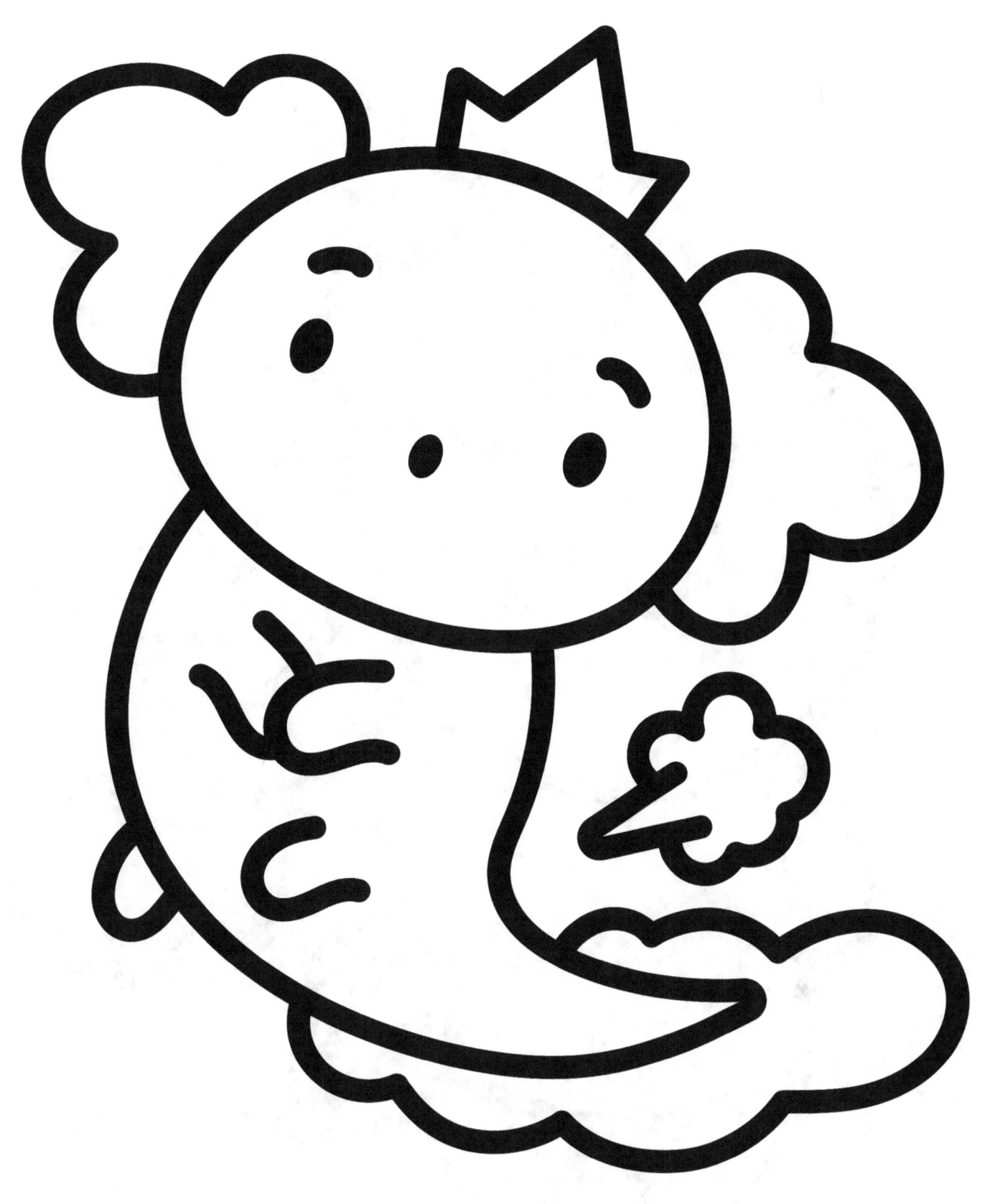

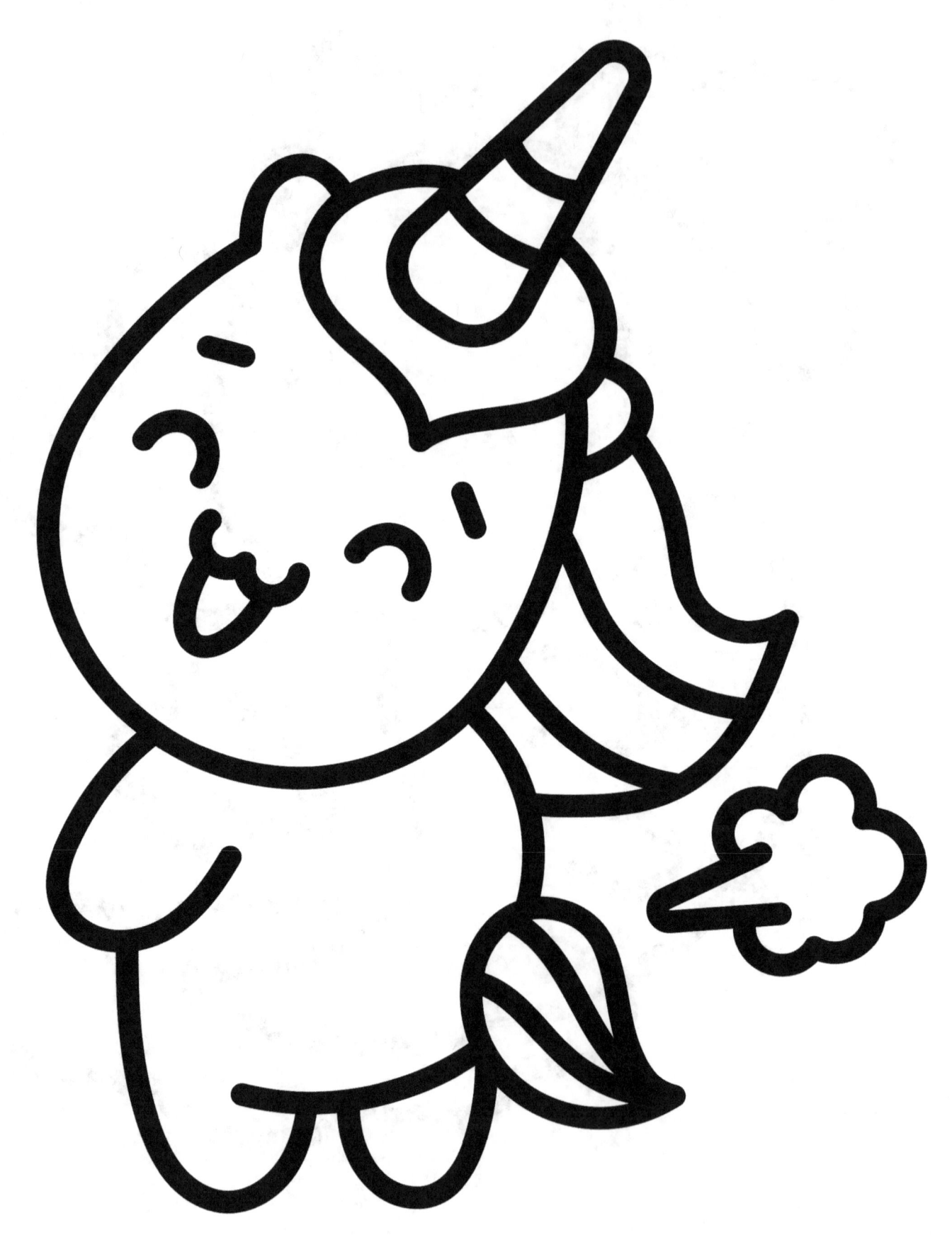

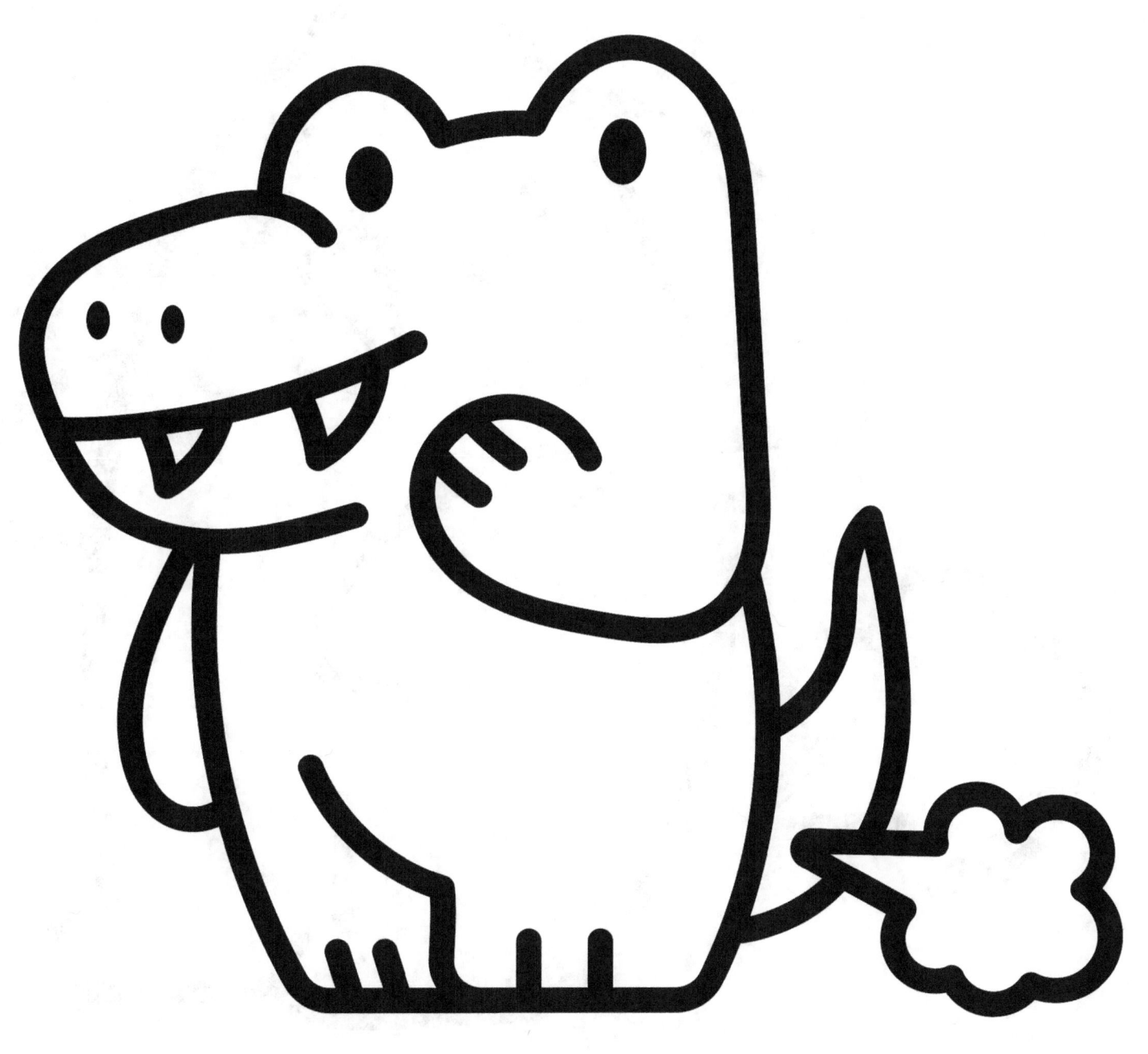

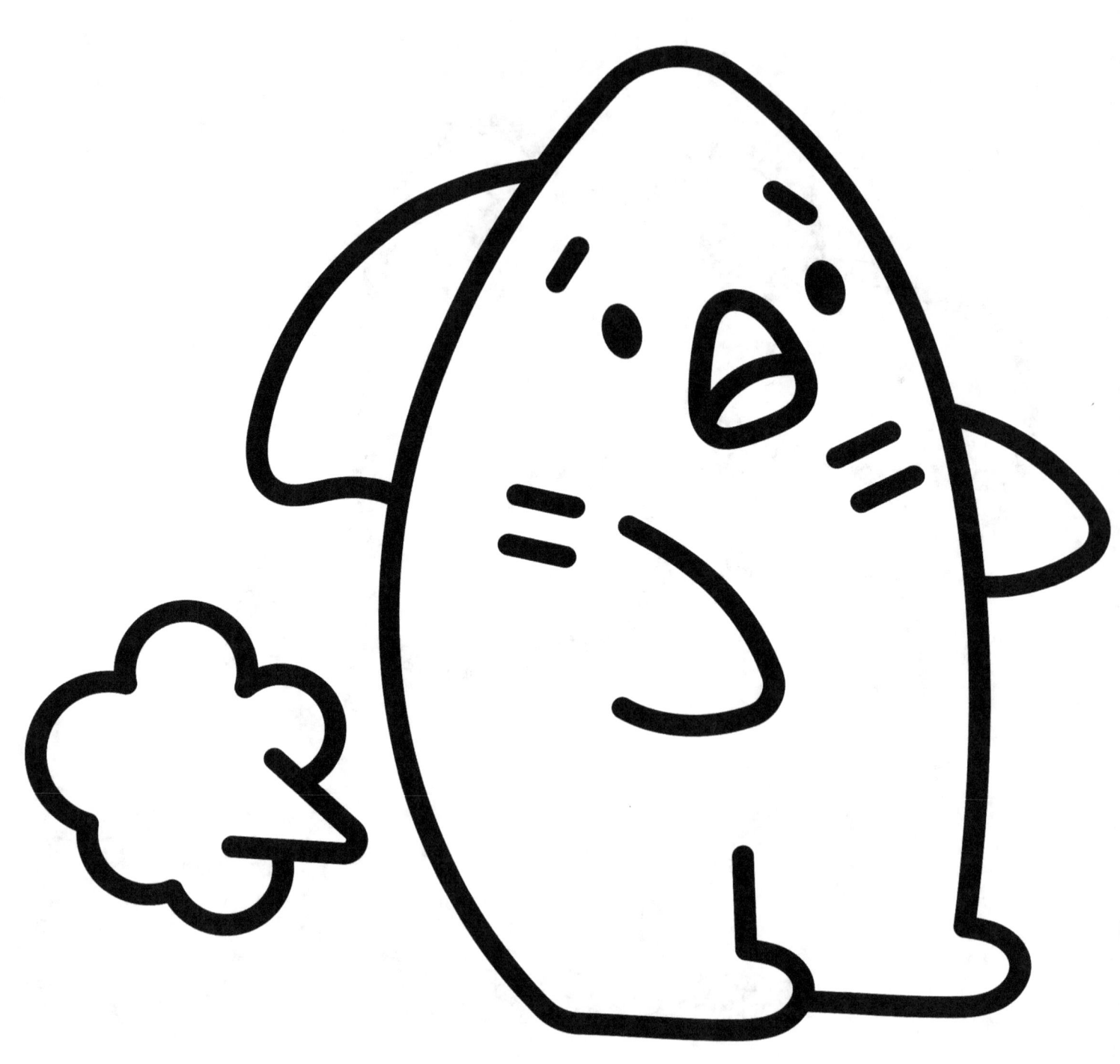

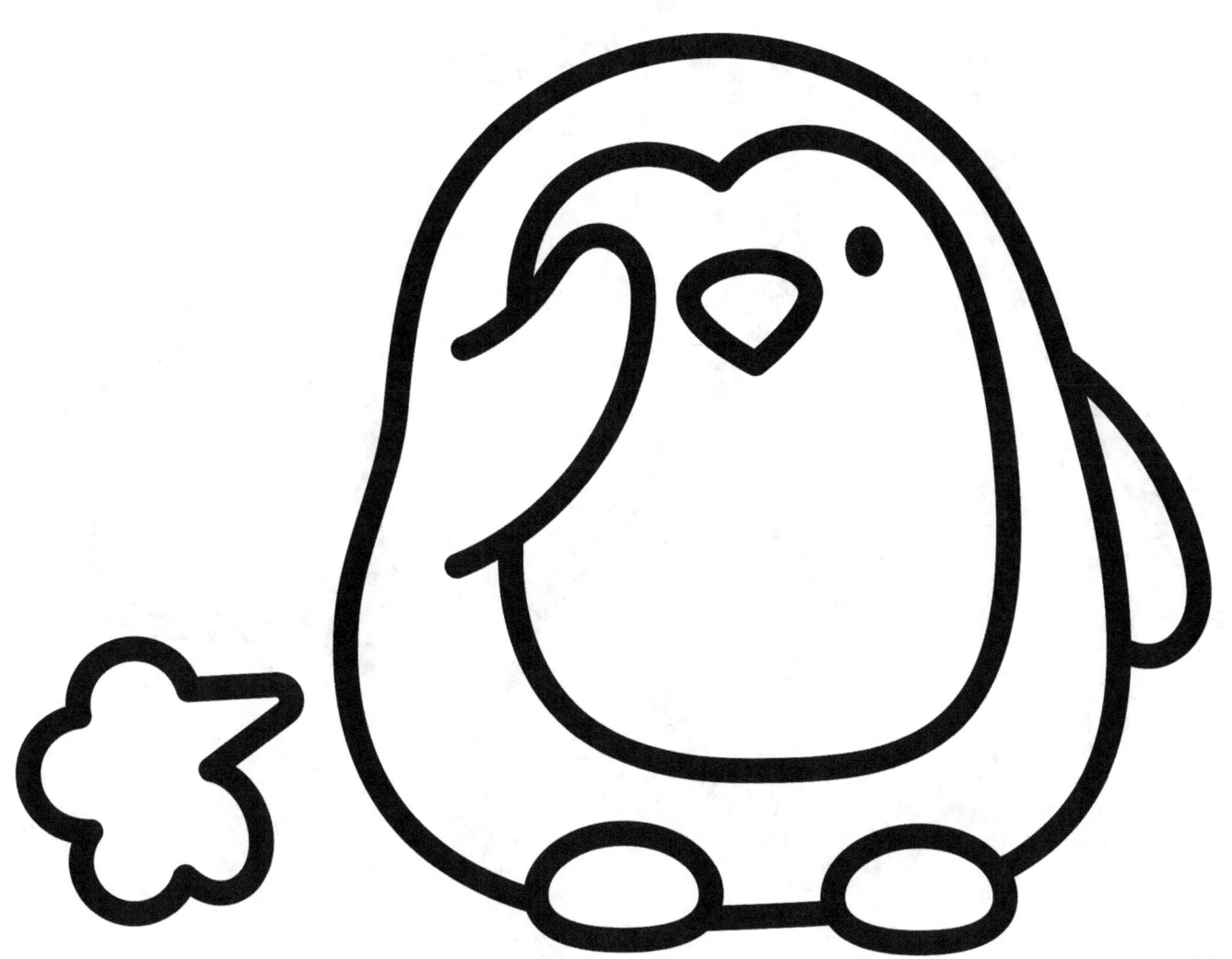

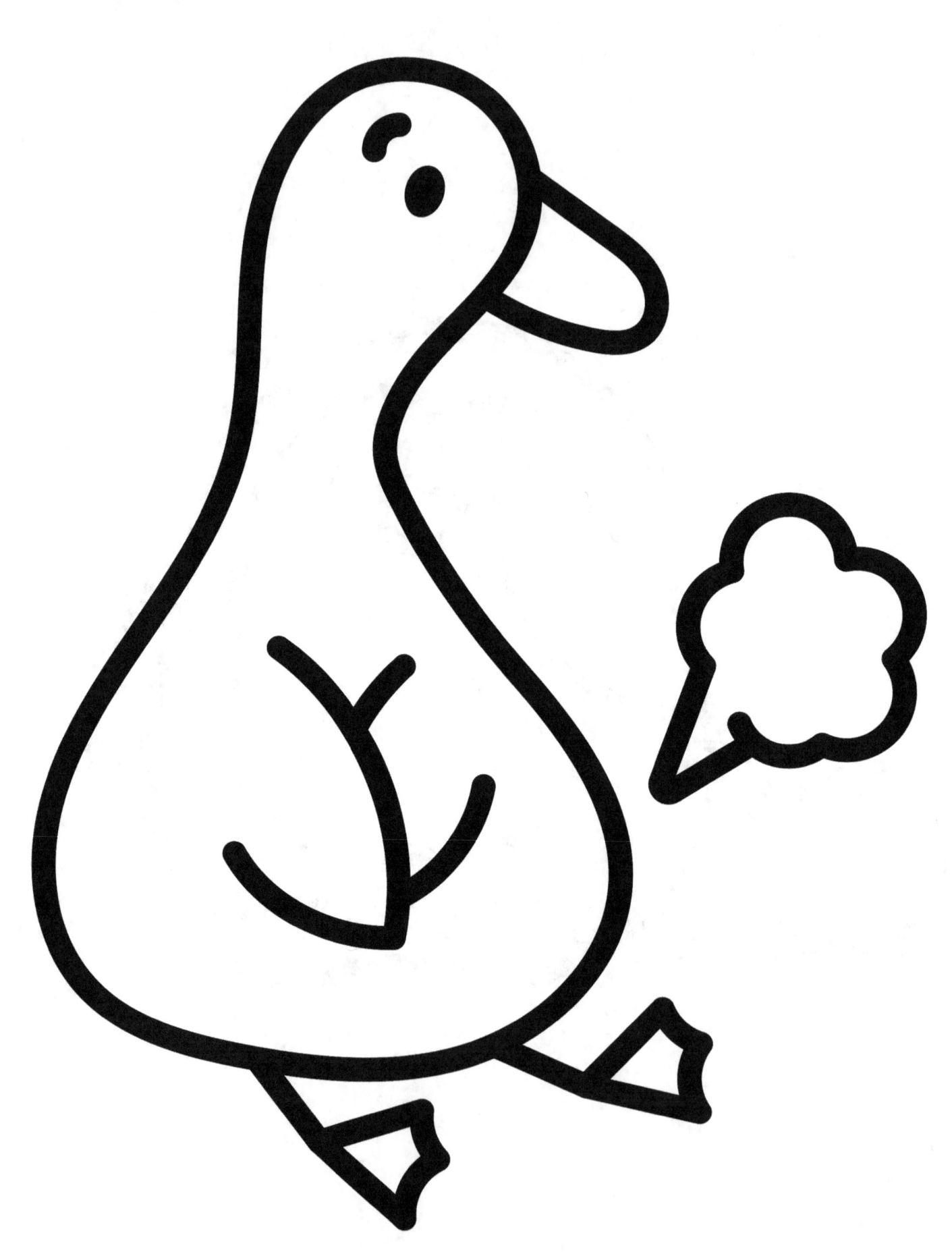

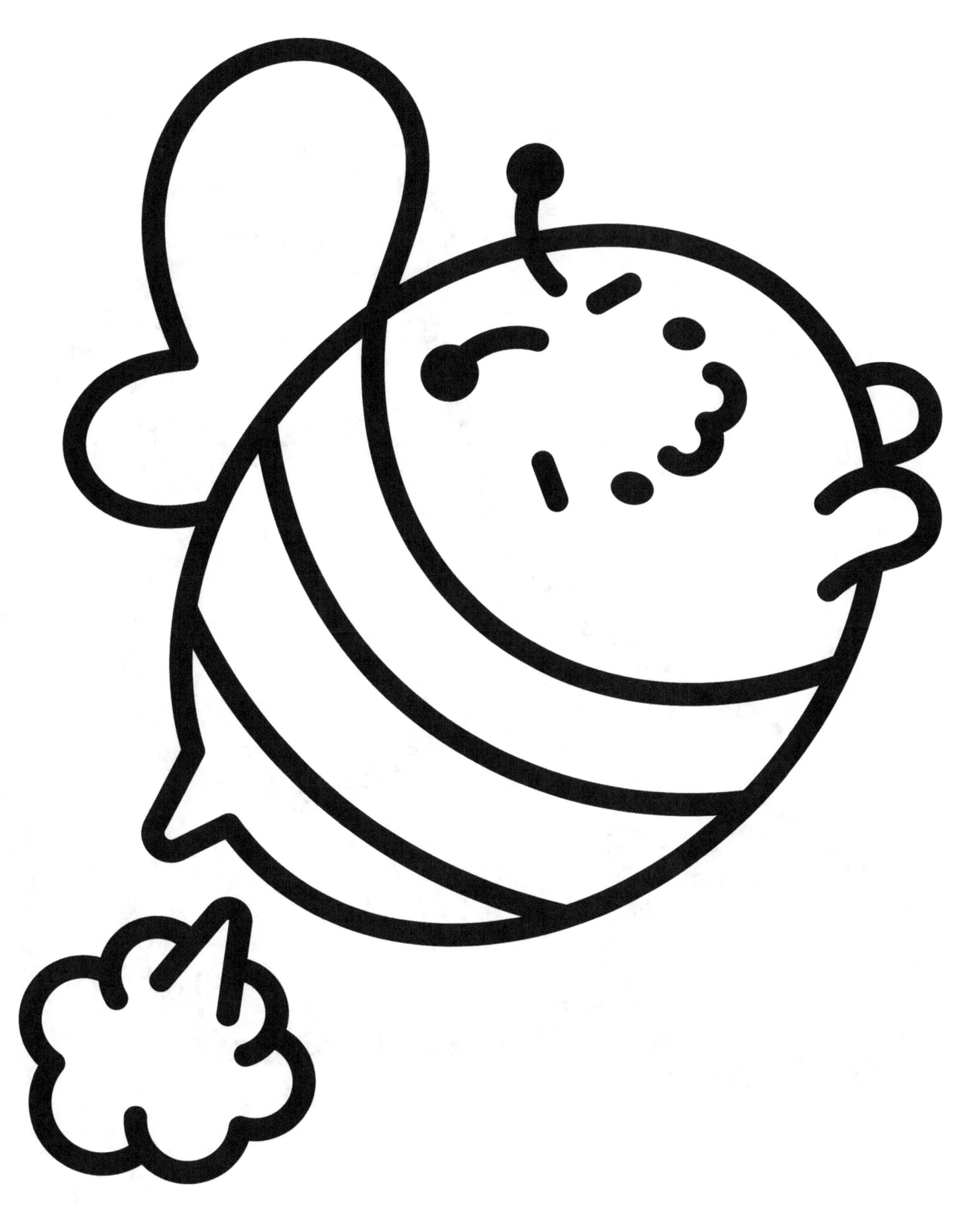

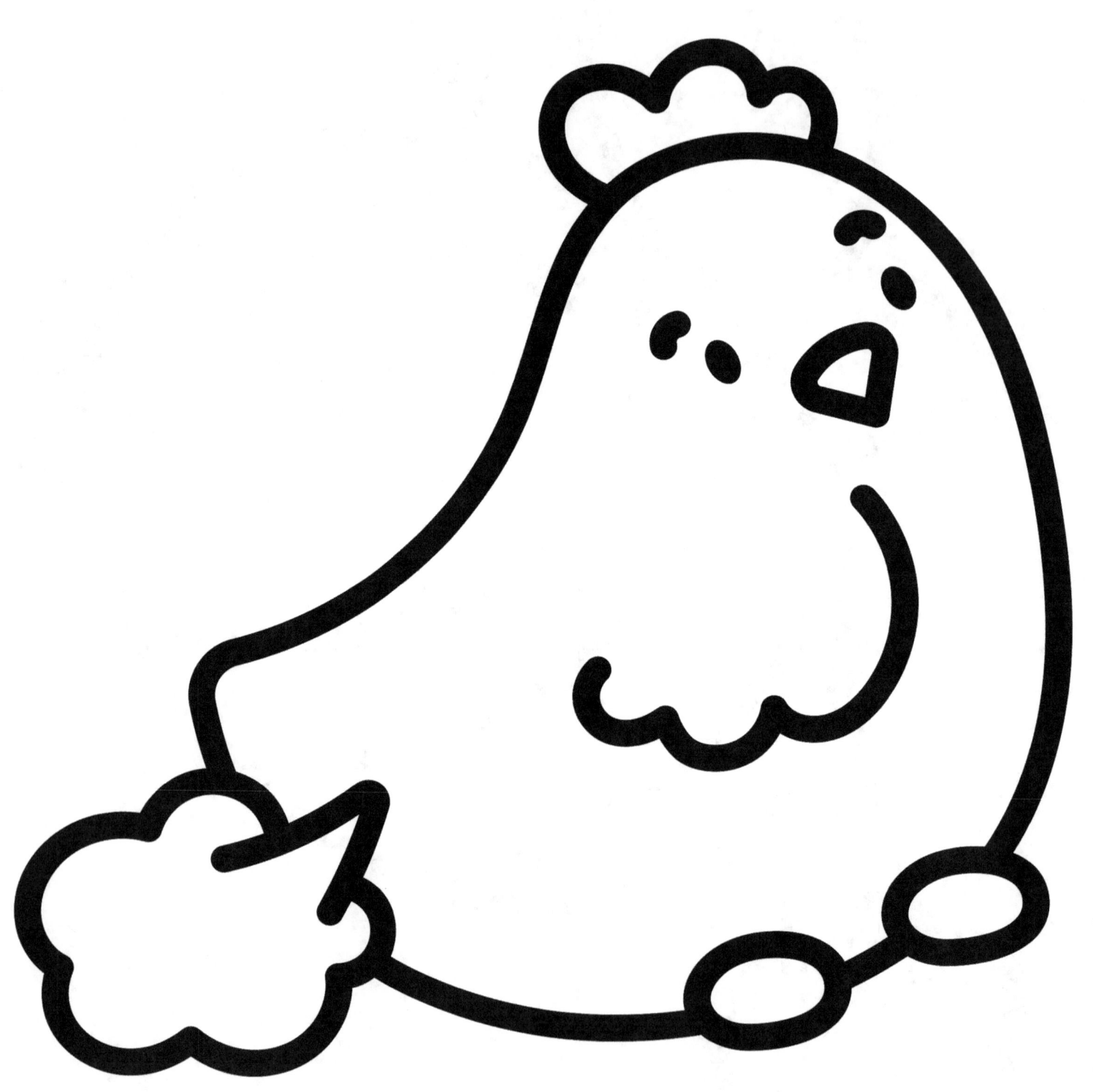

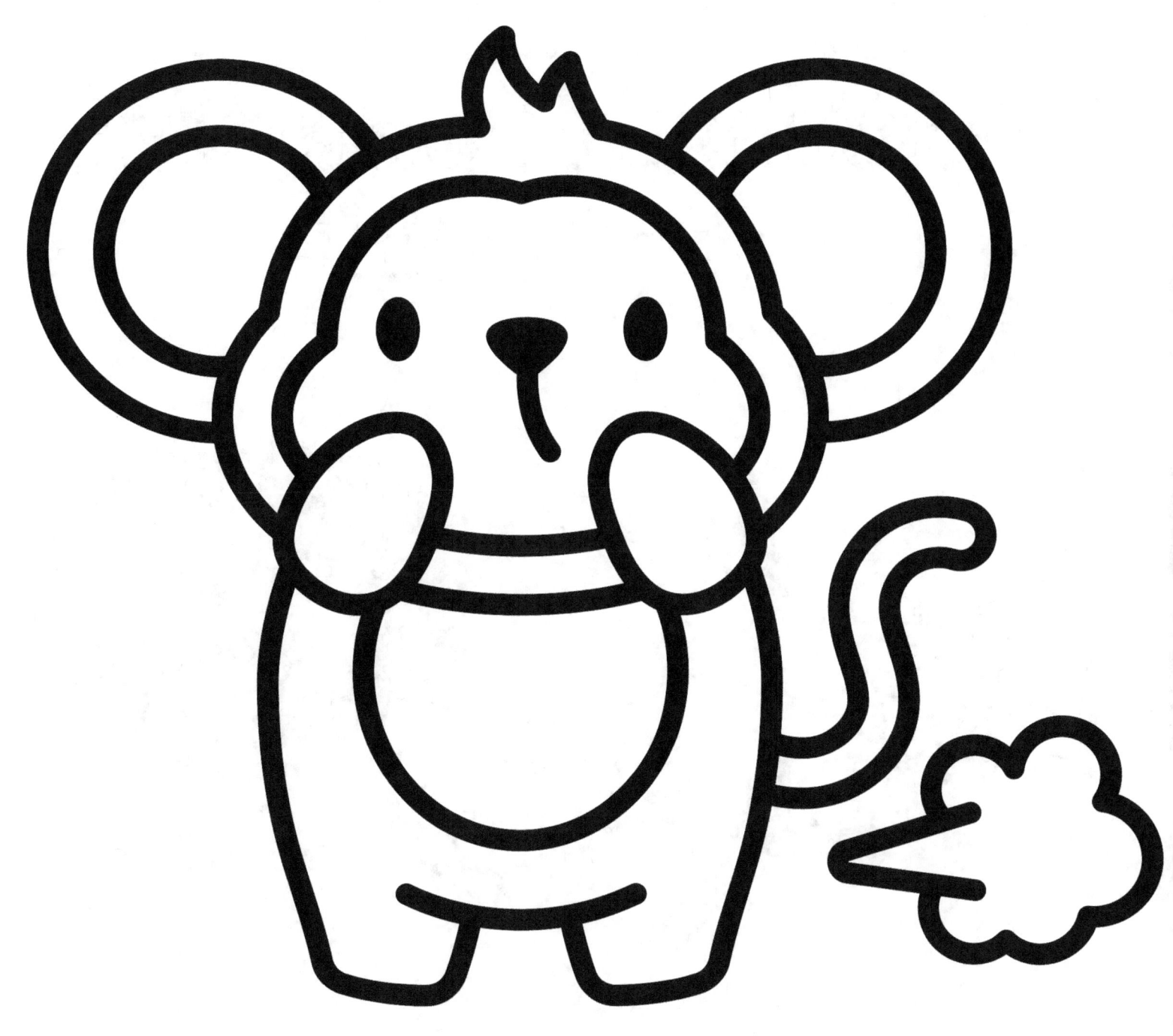

# THAT'S ONE WAY TO ANNOUNCE YOU'RE KING OF THE JUNGLE.

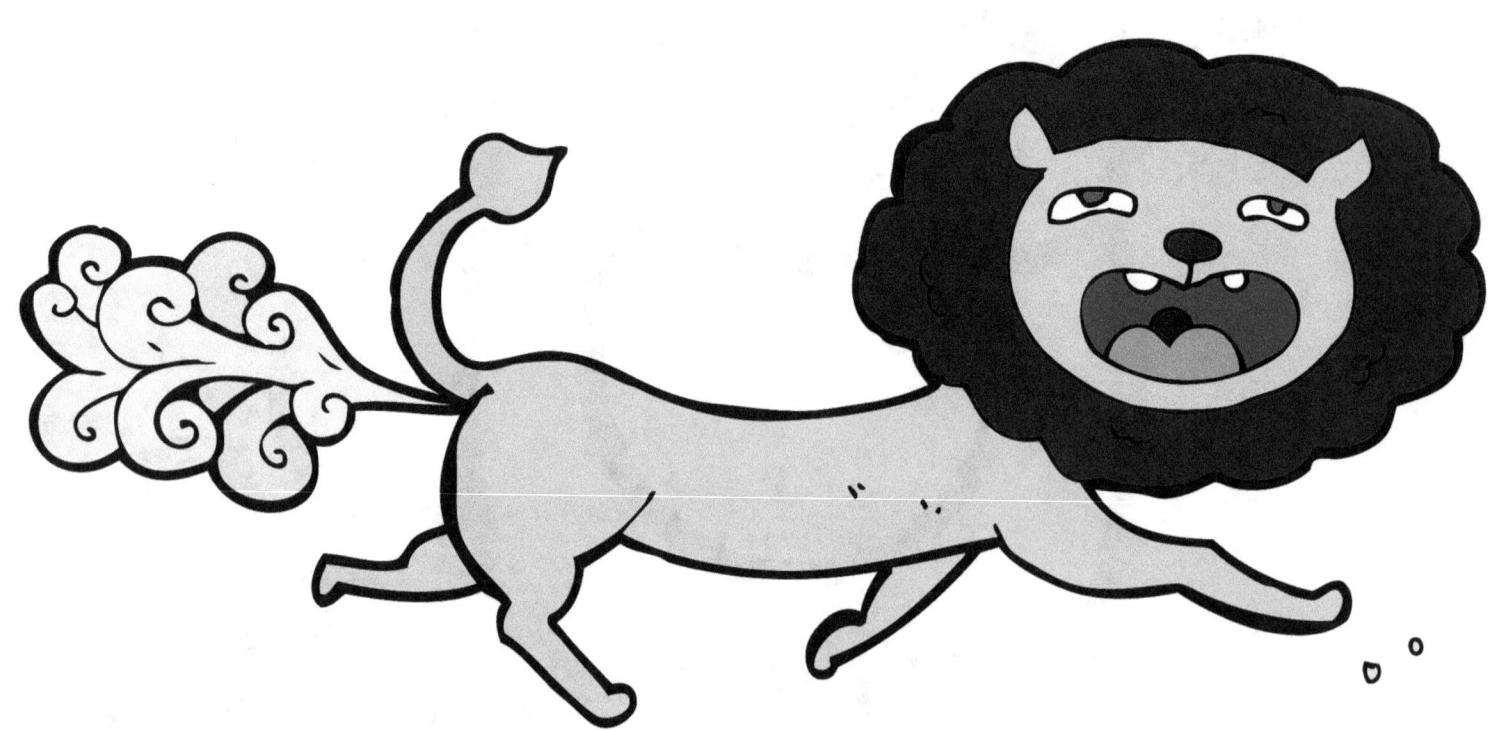

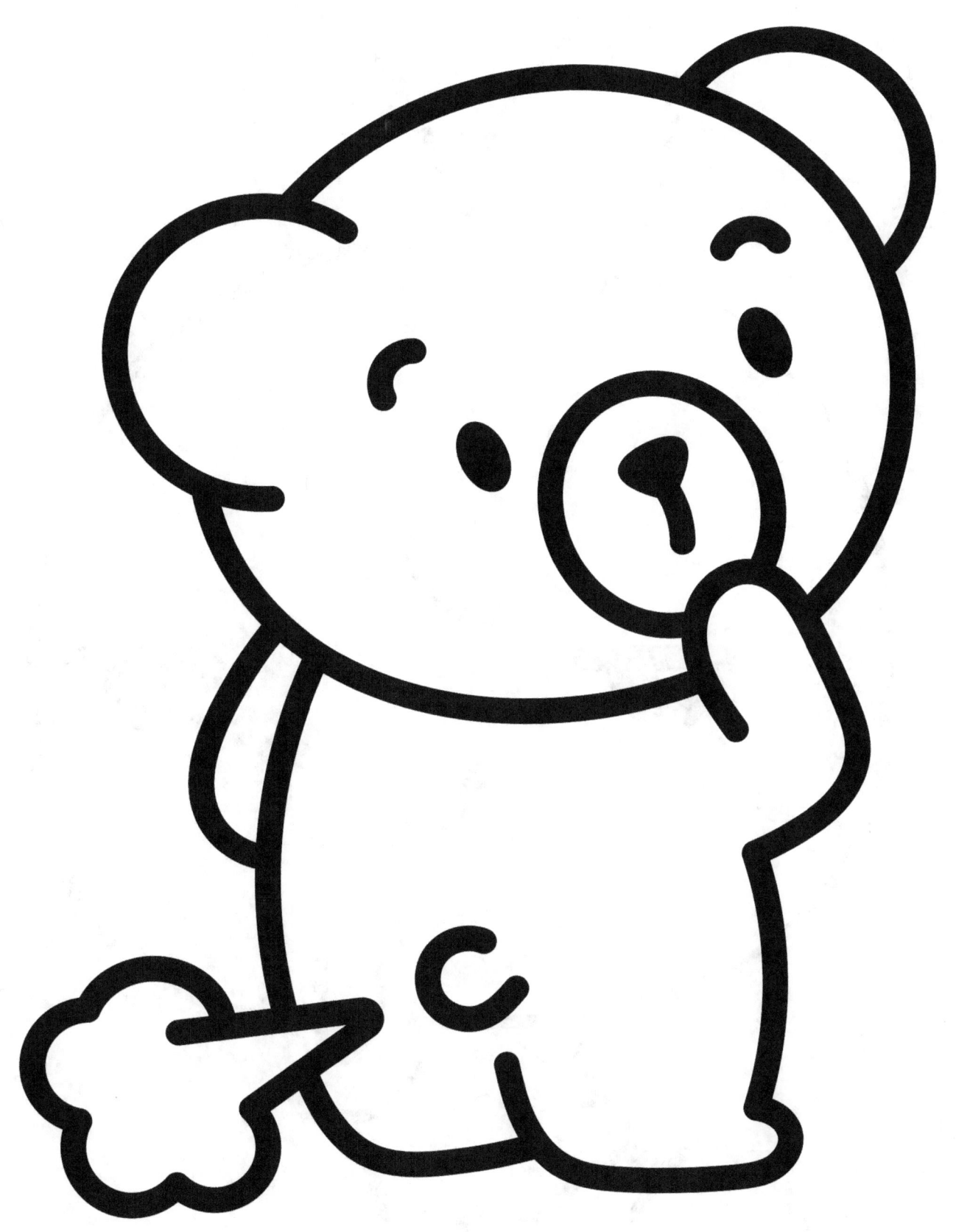

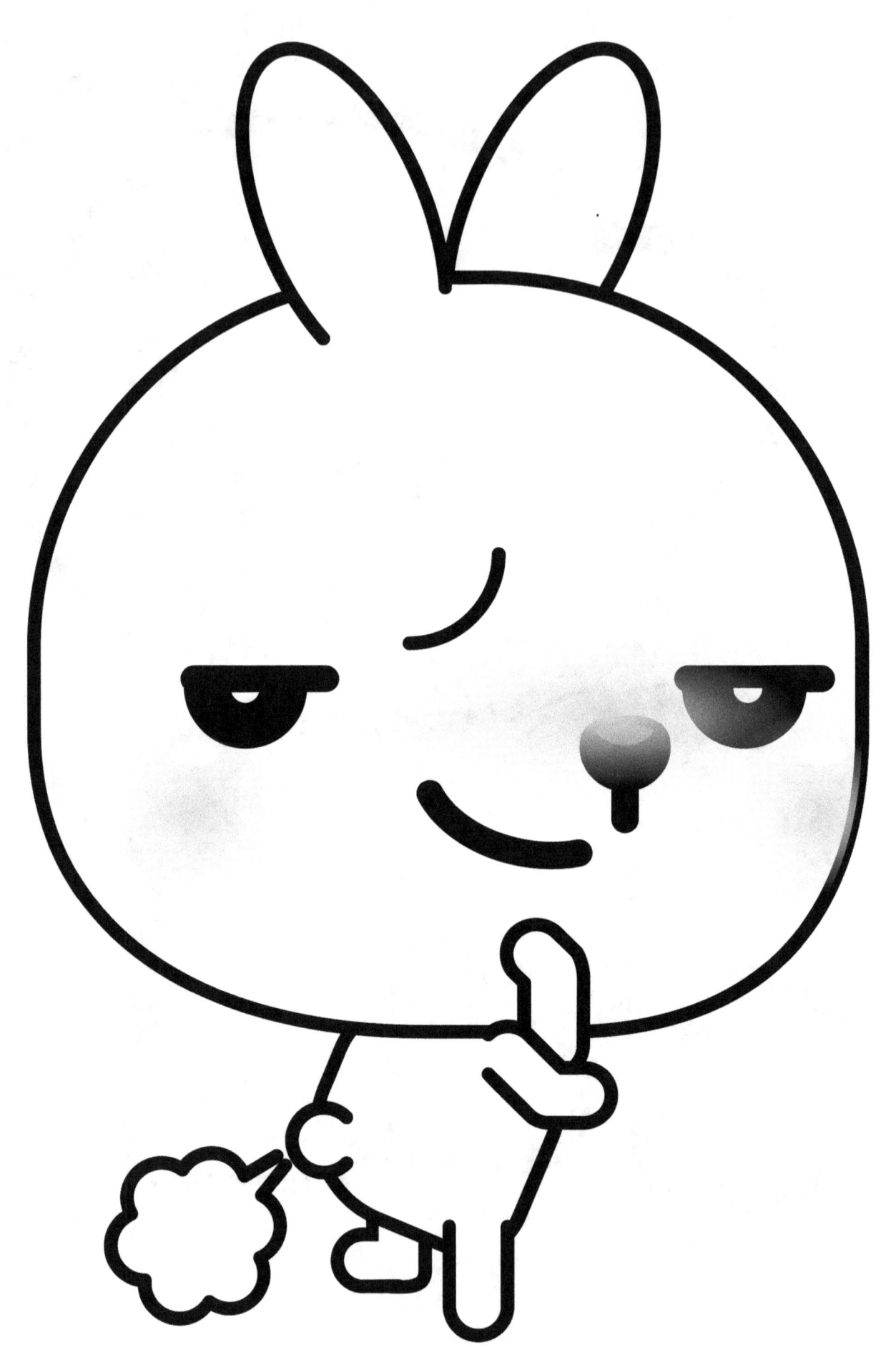

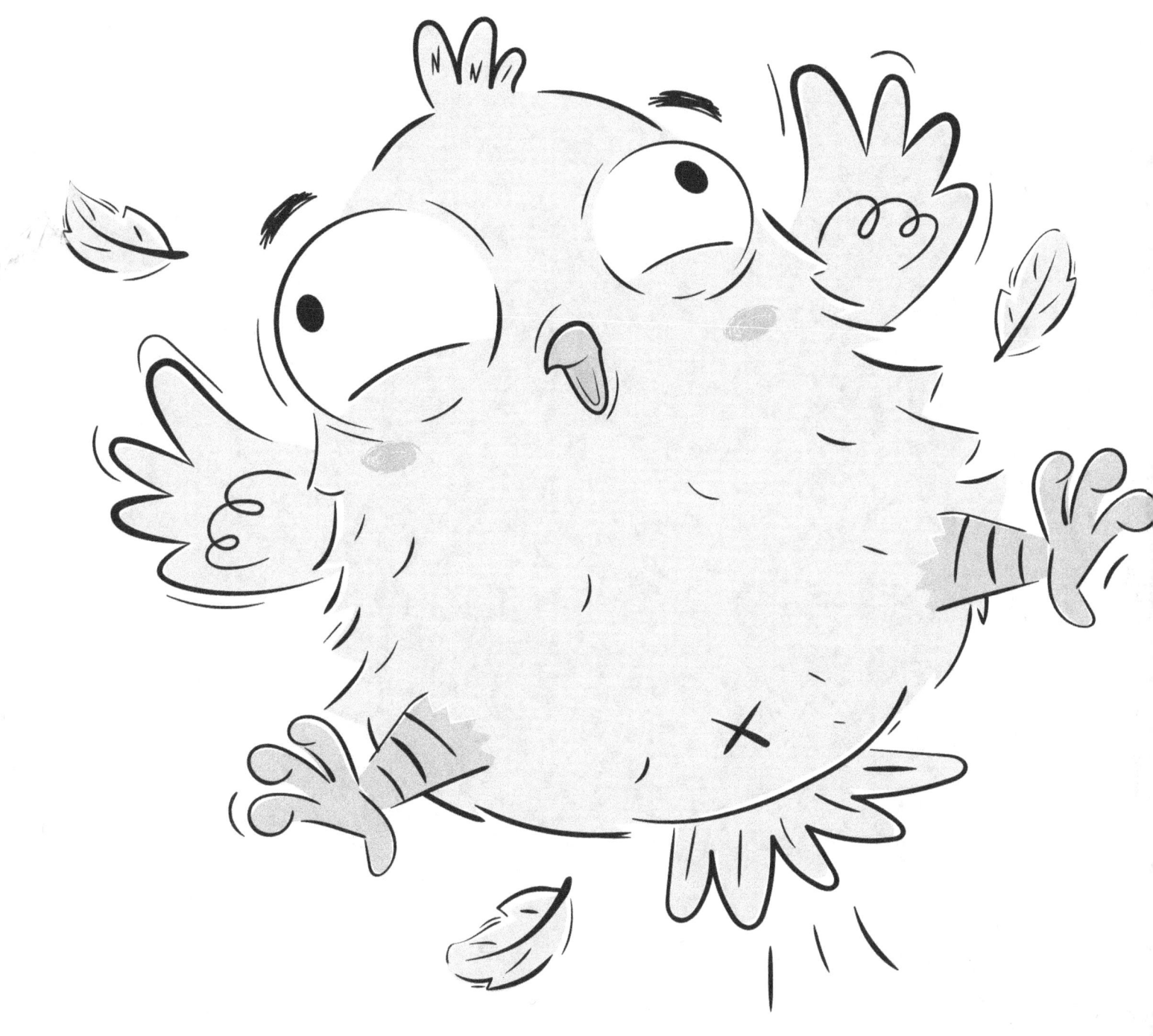

www.ingramcontent.com/pod-product-compliance
Lightning Source LLC
Chambersburg PA
CBHW062224220526
45471CB00009B/3336